A
PRICE GUIDE
TO
BEER ADVERTISING
OPENERS AND CORKSCREWS

by

Donald Bull

Donald A. Bull
20 Fairway Drive
Stamford, CT 06903

Trumbull, Connecticut
1981

Library of Congress Catalogue Card Number 80-70998

ISBN 0-9601190-5-1

Printed in the United States of America

Cover design by Bonnie Bull

Typesetting by Type Plus Graphics, Inc., Stamford, CT

Published by Donald Bull, P.O. Box 106, Trumbull, CT 06611

also by the author . . .

THE REGISTER OF UNITED STATES BREWERIES 1876—1976 (with Manfred Friedrich)

THE REGISTER OF UNITED STATES BREWERIES 1876—1976, Volume II, An Alphabetical Index (with Manfred Friedrich)

BEER ADVERTISING OPENERS—A PICTORIAL GUIDE (1978)

just for openers . . .

When I put together BEER ADVERTISING OPENERS — A PICTORIAL GUIDE in 1978 through the help of a number of dedicated collectors, I considered it to be a fairly complete guide to the types of openers used as a beer advertising medium. There were over 200 different types pictured in that book. Since then I have come to know several hundred opener collectors and over 200 additional types of openers. Pictures of these openers have been included in my quarterly newsletter "Just for Openers."

There are, no doubt, other "types" of beer advertising openers not shown in this book. I have seen thousands of openers in major collections and any new types that turn up could be considered uncommon if not rare (excluding any new ones to be made in the future). There are hundreds of other types with and without advertisements. Advertising openers cover everything from automobiles to funeral homes to zoos. In addition there are many different foreign (to the U.S.) beer advertising types not included in this book.

Corkscrews, can openers, and bottle openers have long been a necessity of life and ingenuity has led to thousands of designs. When I last visited collector Art Santen of St. Louis, Missouri, he had reached the 5,000 mark in his accumulation of all types of openers including state souvenier openers, multi-purpose utensils, canes, etc. — an astonishing assortment. Joe Balaban of Indianapolis, Indiana opened my eyes to the world of corkscrews when he showed me his collection of several hundred varieties. And then there is my wife's collection of cast iron figural openers numbering over 100 in the forms of elephants, donkeys, birds, people, etc. The collector of beer advertising openers should look at all types for additions to his collection — it is surprising what was used. Can you imagine beer advertising on a combination opener and cake server (see Type F-13)? Beer advertising on a combination opener and shoehorn (see Type N-11)? Openers of all types were effective advertising giveaways to keep a product name in front of the public.

Beginning on page 10 over 400 different types of beer advertising openers and corkscrews are pictured and described. The type classification system is the same as used in BEER ADVERTISING OPENERS — A PICTORIAL GUIDE and in "Just for Openers". Each opener is assigned to a letter group — the general classification of the type of opener. Within each general classification there are a number of type variations and each is assigned a number. Assignments of numbers to variations of a given style are only made when the difference is significant. If a collector were to accumulate thousands of type "I" openers and make comparisons of lengths, widths, manufacturers' names, piercing points, position of ends in relation to one another, and other minor details, he would probably come up with over 100 types. As another example, in the C-12 and C-15 types there might be another 50 varieties. Depicting varieties not readily noticeable would only lead to a nightmare in classifying one's finds. If you have an opener which comes very close to the type shown, that is the type. If it is easily recognized as different, let me know about it so it can be assigned a type classification.

The openers shown in the Guide to Values are approximately 30 percent of actual size - actual measurements are indicated in the descriptions.

Except for the Type P corkscrews, the type descriptions facing each photo page are in numerical sequence. The reason the openers do not appear in numerical order on the photo pages is because numbers were assigned as new types were submitted to me for inclusion in "Just for Openers". Similar styles have been placed next to their close relatives (except type M and N which are in numerical order). For example on page 15 you will find types C-5 and C-28 next to each other.

The values shown are based on average dollar buying and selling prices at flea markets, antique shows, auctions, and collector get-togethers. Some openers are quite rare in the collections known to me and as a result, would command rather high prices. You may get lucky as many collectors have and happen upon what is considered a rare opener for 5¢ at a garage sale and the next time you see it in an antique show it may be ten or fifteen dollars. Also it has happened that a hoard of a given type is discovered and the market prices plummet. I recall paying $15.00 for my first Type M-1 Pickwick Beer opener several years ago. A couple of years later hundreds of them turned up in Massachusetts at prices ranging from $2.00 to $5.00. The supply now seems to be exhausting and the price is on the way up — it is all in the realm of that old law of "supply and demand." The beer advertising opener and corkscrew collector must keep in mind that there are others in addition to just plain beer advertising opener collectors who are scavenging about in flea markets and antique shows for the same things — openers with a particular brand of beer advertised that interests him, corkscrews for the collector of all types of corkscrews, openers for the utensil collector, knives with openers on the blades for the knife collector, and openers for use in opening bottles or cans!

Sometimes you will pay more than the values shown in this book. Sometimes you will pay less. If you see an opener you like and you feel the price is satisfactory, buy it — you may never see it again. When I first started collecting, I passed up a type R-5 shark with Schlitz logo at $12.50. I've been trying to find another ever since.

On the following pages I am presenting some information of significant developments in beer advertising corkscrews and openers. Throughout the descriptions in the Guide to Values you will find more historical information and many references to patent dates on openers. If you can contribute any additional information on any of the openers shown, please let me know.

Donald Bull
P.O. Box 106
Trumbull, CT 06611

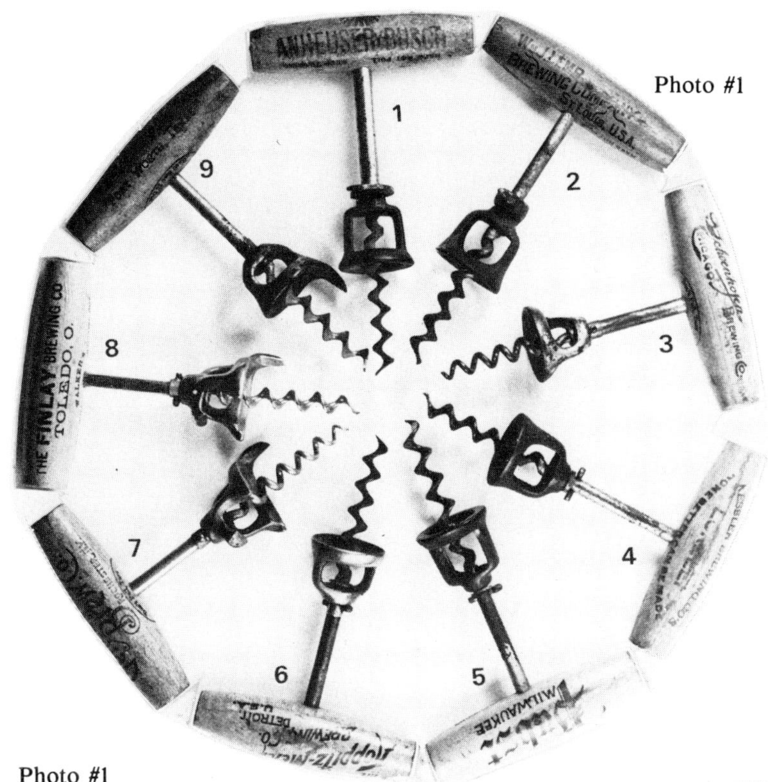

Prior to the invention of the crimped bottle cap, breweries used corks which were secured by wire or string to the bottle thereby protecting the precious brew inside. The practice of wiring or tying the cork was the rule, rather than the exception. For half a century the corkscrew was the opener for beer as well as medicines, various commercial waters, inks, photographic liquids, whiskey and wine. The bottle cap did not become commercially usable until the 1890s. Eighteen wood handled corkscrews are shown here. None of these corkscrews are alike although differences may be slight and only caught by the watchful eye. Reference is to form rather than advertising. Additional corkscrews and information on corkscrews appear under "P Types" on page 34-37.

Photo #1

#1 & #2: A William A. Williamson design patent #D29,798 of Dec. 13, 1898. The cast wire cutter/cap lifter above the bell is the patented part.

#3 & #6: An Edwin Walker patent #501,975 of July 25, 1893. The brass sleeve which the bell rotates around was the patented part.

#4 & #5: Williamson patent #587,900 of Aug. 10, 1897. The small washer separating the bell and cotter pin was the patented part.

#7 & #8: Walker patent #647,775 of April 17, 1900. The cast bell incorporating wire breaker and cap lifter was the patented part.

#9   : Walker patent #579,200 of March 23, 1897. A design patent was issued on July 14, 1896 (#D25,776). The cast wire breaker was the patent.

Photo #2

#1 is the Walker patent #579,200 referred to above with a cap lifter/wire breaker inserted into one end of the wooden handle.

#2 is the Walker patent #501,975 (above) with wire breaker/cap lifter.

#3 is the Williamson patent #587,900 (above) with wire breaker in handle.

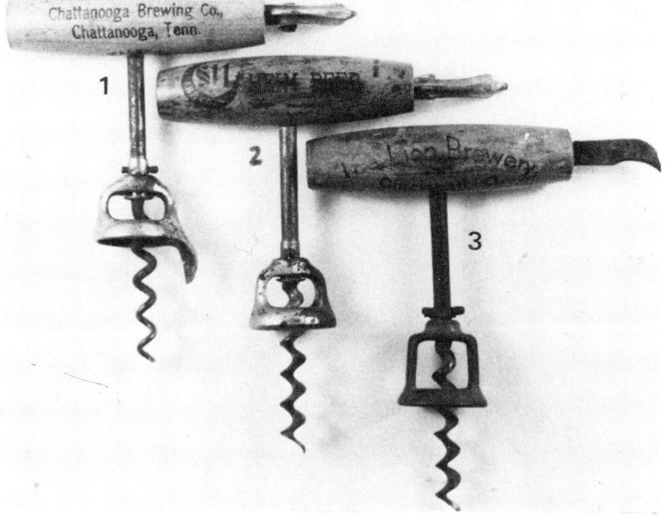

Photo #2

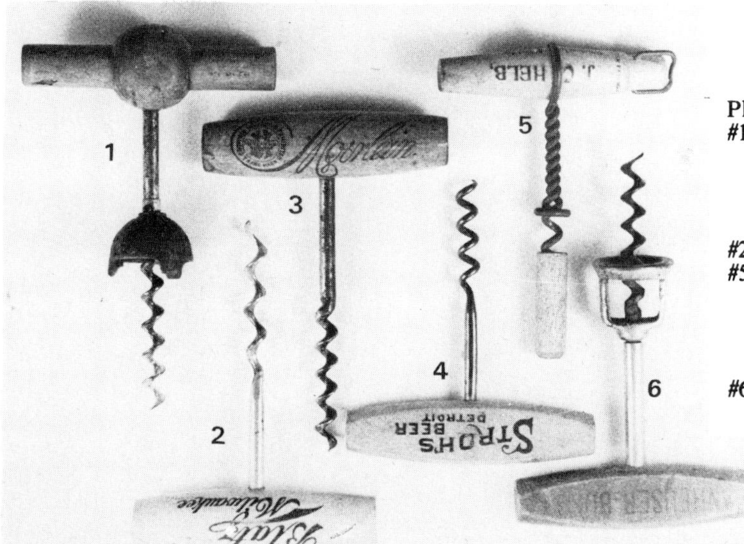

Photo #3

Photo #3

#1 is a relatively rare wooden handled corkscrew produced by the Erie Specialty Manufacturing Co. (1888-1891). This corkscrew is an excellent example of what was to become known as the "Self-puller" (1893), a patent by Edwin Walker of Erie, Pennsylvania.

#2, #3, and #4 were made by Williamson Co. of Newark, N.J.

#5 Corkscrews with wooden handles and twisted steel wire were made from 1876 through the 1920s. This particular example has a cap lifter attached to the end of the handle. This device was patented in the U.S. as a "Decapitator" on March 1, 1910, patent #950,509.

#6 Made by the Williamson Co. of Newark, N.J. after 1897.

The development of the cap lifter, by necessity, occurred at the same time as the introduction of the crown cap. In 1892 William Painter of Baltimore, Maryland invented the crown cap. He was granted a patent on Feb. 6, 1894 for his simple cap lifter design. The patent application papers of June 5, 1893 illustrate an opener similar to type D-6 (see pages 16-17). Walker, Williamson, and others quickly took heed of this new development and incorporated cap lifters into their corkscrews designs as shown on the preceding page. Walker was later an important factor in the development of the wire formed openers (Type E) which were produced by the millions in a number of variations from about 1910 through the 70's. Walker originally filed his patent papers in September of 1909. By taking suitable lengths of rod or wire drawn from a coil and forming them into shapes shown below in the patent drawings, a crown opener could be produced very inexpensively. In a 1976 Vaughan Mfg. Co. price list wire bottle openers with imprinting were available at $35.50 per thousand in 10,000 quantity lots or less than one-half cent each.

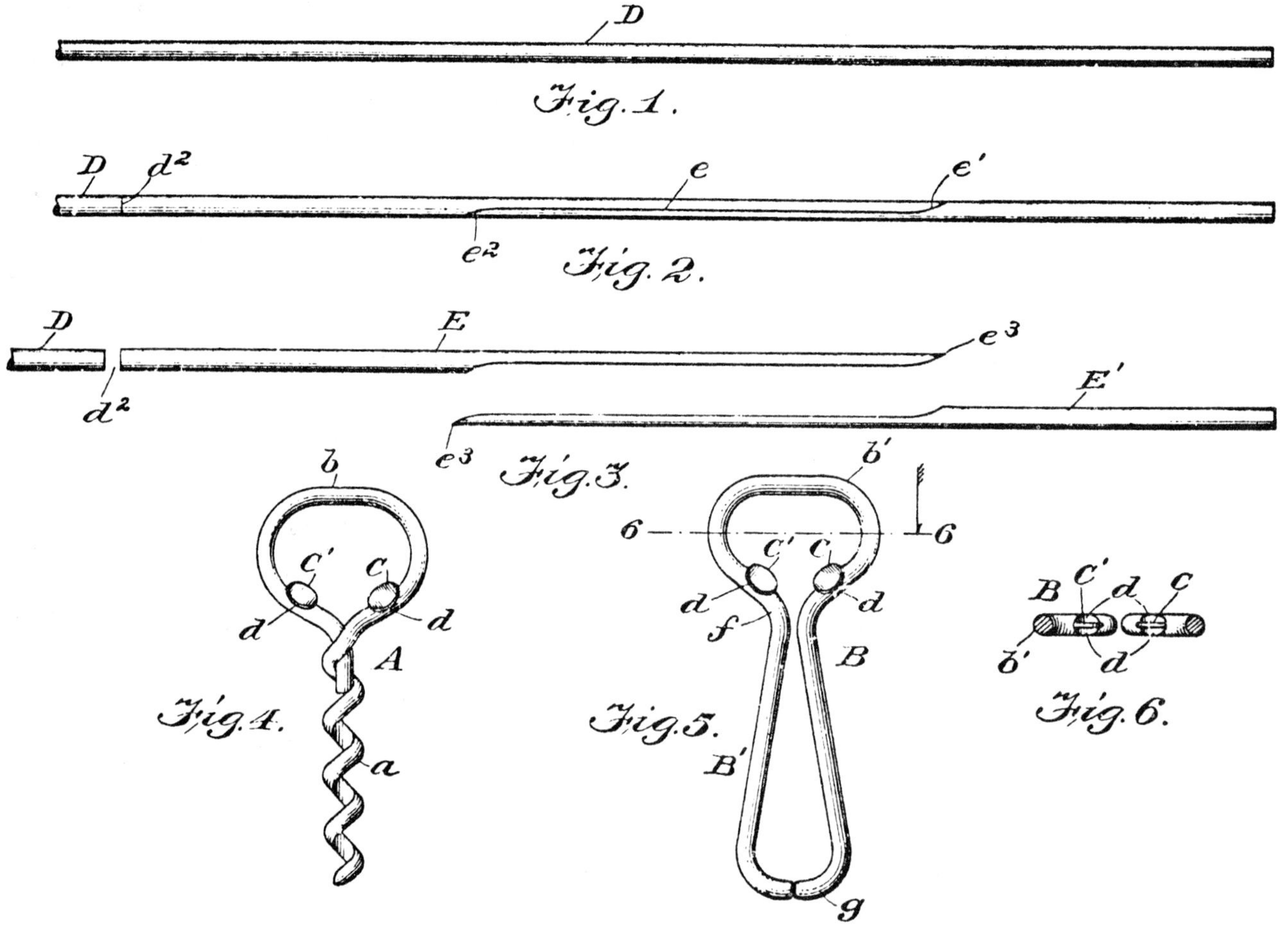
Fig. 1.
Fig. 2.
Fig. 3.
Fig. 4.
Fig. 5.
Fig. 6.

Many variations of pocket type cap lifters (Types A & B) were introduced in the 1900-1915 period and were designed with holes for placing them on key chains with other "keys." Some of these styles continued during prohibition (officially 1920-1933) and were practically phased out of the market by the combination cap lifter and can opener introduced in the 30's. Notable exceptions are Types A-12, A-20, A-39, and B-24. John L. Sommer of Newark, New Jersey, Augustus W. Stephens of Cambridge, Mass. and Harry Vaughan of Chicago, Illinois were important figures in the design of these openers. Some of their patent design numbers and dates are listed in the descriptions of A and B type openers. It is interesting to note that although the 18th Amendment (Prohibition) became effective in January of 1920, some A & B type openers showing beer advertisements appear in a 1922 Vaughan Novelty Manufacturing Co. catalog. They were only depicting styles available in their line, and their primary business at that time was with concerns producing soft drinks and near beer. A cut from the Vaughan catalog is shown at right.

Vaughan Novelty Mfg. Co.

O-U-T-I-N-G KEY STYLE — No. 12

POCKET BOTTLE OPENER

Schlitz
OUTING
IN
BROWN
BOTTLES

"Finished the Vaughan Way."

Polished and Double Plated.

Packed in Boxes of 100.

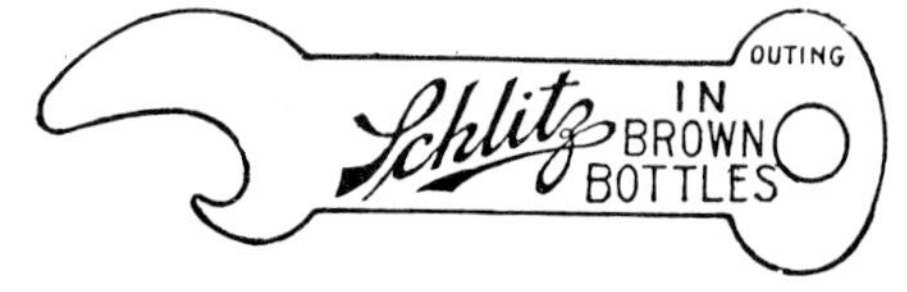

Quantity	250	500	1000	2500	5000	10,000
Price	**$6.50**	**10.00**	**18.00**	**17.00**	**16.00**	**15.00 M.**

On January 16, 1919 the 18th Amendment to the Constitution of the United States was ratified and one year later the manufacture, sale, and transport of intoxicating liquors was prohibited by law. This act had a devastating affect on the brewing industry. In 1914 there were approximately 1250 breweries in operation. Only about 600 of these resumed production of legalized beer after the repeal of prohibition in 1933. Obviously, the market for "beer advertising openers" was also wiped out by the act. There were openers produced with other advertising but the beer advertising opener collector will have to do without real beer openers for that 14 year period.

In 1932 several "openers" appeared on the market in the form of a caricature of Andrew Volstead. Volstead was a member of Congress when the 18th Amendment was introduced and was responsible for a bill which provided the mechanism for federal enforcement of the act. The Prohibition Act was often referred to as the "Volstead Act." Because he is remembered as the "Father of the Prohibition Act," we can also place the blame on him for the decline in the number of breweries and the prohibition period gap in beer advertising openers. Volstead openers belong in a beer advertising opener collection.

The openers shown in the photo below are as follows:
1. Volstead on a camel. The cap lifter is the handle of his umbrella. It is marked "Prohibition, The End of the Trail, Copyright 1933."
2. The rarest of the Volstead openers. Has cap lifter on front and back of head and corkscrew in back. Bronze.
3. Brass or chrome plated pot metal Volstead with corkscrew. Top hat removes to expose hole for possibly concealing illegal intoxicants!
4. Nickel plated corkscrew and cap lifter. Head turns to raise corkscrew.

The top of the casket to the right is labelled "Born 1919, Died_______." A corkscrew is attached to the top hat. Volstead's stomach, the barrel, is a jigger. The turned up toes serve as a cap lifter and on top of the leg is a cork for resealing a bottle. A slip of paper in the casket states that "Mr. Prohibition has 'gone to pieces'." and includes this verse:

Poor Mr. Prohibition's licked —
  We've got him on his back!
He's trying hard to make amends
  Before he's in "the sack".

Let's look him over just for fun,
  He may be used at that!
There's nothing in that head of his —
  He's "screwy" in the hat!

His stomach now is changed a bit —
  It measures out the rye.
A "Jigger-ful" each time it's used!
  Say! He's a useful guy!

He kicks off caps with utmost ease
  We've got his cork in spirit!
And when he passes on, dear friend —
  We know that we can "beer-it"!

During Prohibition Harry Vaughan introduced his "Over the Top" style opener. Vaughan applied for his patent in 1921 and the patent was issued in 1924. The sheet metal opener is "formed substantially complete in a single stamping operation." The opener was produced by taking a strip of metal and "the same being first stamped out in the form of a blank of proper conformation and then bent into ultimate form by means of suitable dies, such conformation being chiefly . . . flanges . . . extending around the edges of a body portion . . . and serving chiefly to reinforce the device against bending when pressure is applied to the handle in the operation of removing the cap." A cut from the 1922 Vaughan catalog illustrates this opener. This was a very popular advertising opener just after the repeal of Prohibition. They were manufactured by Vaughan in Chicago and G.G. Greene Co. in Warren, Pa. In 1928 C. Hiering of Newark, New Jersey added a folding corkscrew to the underside of this opener and his patent was assigned to the J.E. Mergott Company for manufacture.

On Feb. 27, 1933 Henry J. Edlund of Burlington, Vermont patented a cap lifter with wood handle available in a variety of colors with advertising imprint in a second color (see Type G-9 on 21). Edlund was prepared for the post-Prohibition "boom" in the beer advertising opener market. Less than 50 different advertisements have been noted on the Edlund opener and most of these were for Eastern brewers.

On January 24, 1935 the first beer in cans was produced. The beer was from the Krueger Brewing Co. of Newark, New Jersey and the can was produced by American Can Company. A brochure from Krueger introducing the beer contains a section showing how to serve and open cans (at right). The can piercer had already been invented (1932) for opening other containers with liquid but the demand now was significantly increased. Can piercers became a necessity of life and were given away by the millions by vendors of beer and other drinks in cans. Initially American Can Company manufactured openers in Newark, New Jersey and during the period 1935-1936 licensed Vaughan Manufacturing to produce the openers as well. During the ensuing boom years for the can opener, Vaughan was by far the largest producer. Others included Handy Walden, Ekco, Emro, Mira, and Greene.

In 1962 Pittsburgh Brewing Co. introduced a can with a pull tab which required no "opener." That and the introduction of the twist off bottle cap signalled the virtual end of beer advertising openers as a mass market item. In recent years there have been a number of "novelty" beer advertising openers produced for special promotional purposes and they are as collectable as the openers produced during the "boom" years.

It is up to you, the collector, to preserve this bit of Americana . . . build your collection . . . just for openers . . .

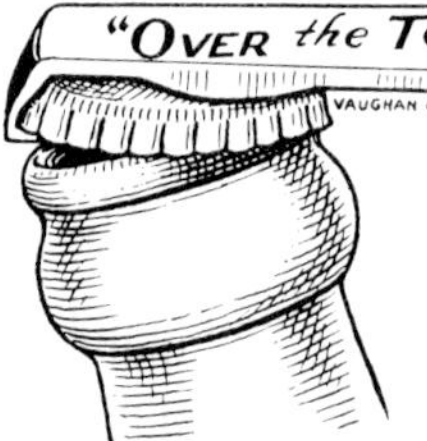

GUIDE TO VALUES

Values for each type are given in ranges (e.g. Type C-16; $2.00 - 5.00). The low value end is for openers from large national brewers and brands such as Pabst, Schlitz, and Coors. These companies produced a lot of beer and their advertising budgets were large — they bought tens of thousands of openers while the smaller brewers settled for hundreds and thousands. Middle value is for regional brands such as Schaefer, Rheingold, and Narragansett. The high end is for brands from small local brewers such as Hull (Connecticut), Schuster (Minnesota), and Bosch (Michigan).

Values are based on openers in good condition with fully legible advertising and minimal rust and pitting.

Values are only for openers and corkscrews which advertise beer unless otherwise indicated.

It is very difficult to assign a value to an opener which might be purchased at a garage sale for 5ᶜ and later found on sale at an antique show for ten or fifteen dollars. The values in this book are only guidelines for the collector and dealer and not necessarily a recommended buy or sell price.

TYPE A FIGURAL OPENERS

A-1   2 7/8″   Female figure wading in water. Some marked "Pat'd"; others marked "C.T.& O. Co. Pat'd. Chicago." A pre-prohibition beer opener. It is shown in a 1922 Vaughan Novelty Mfg. Co. catalog in two styles: clothed (Bathing Girl) and nude (Mermaid design). 1922 advertisers costs ranged from $6.50 for 250 to $15.00 per thousand in 10,000 quantity.   10-15

A-2   3″   Nude female figure pouring contents of bottle into glass. This type has been noted with bar and club names but not with a beer name.   10

A-3   3 1/8″   Girl in bathing suit and cap. This type has been reported with names of several malt companies and malt products but no beer name.   12

A-4 and A-5   2 3/4″   Both types depict either a nude girl (Early Morn) or a clothed girl (Calendar Girl). Type A-4 has a square hole (Prest-O-Lite Key) used as a wrench to open a valve on carbide tanks on the running boards of autos. When the valve was opened, it furnished gas for the headlights. A-5 does not have the square hole. Design Patent No. 44,226 was granted on June 17, 1913 to Harry L. Vaughan and assigned to Crown Throat and Opener Company of Chicago (C.T.&O. Co).   8-10

A-6   2 3/4″   This lady's leg and shoe has only been reported with advertising for West End Brewing Co. of Utica, New York.   10

A-7 and A-35   Fancy lady's boot marked "Pat'd Mar. 12, 1912." (Design Patent No. 42,306 to John L. Sommer). A-7 does not have the square hole. A-35 does.   12-15

A-8   2 3/4″   This double cap lifter depicts a bespectacled gentleman with uniform and was probably made exclusively as an advertising piece for Jacob Ruppert Knickerbocker Beer of New York.   20

A-9   3 1/8″   Baseball player with hands held overhead in throwing position. The key chain hole represents the ball. Marked "Pat'd 8-18-14." (Design Patent No. 43,298 to John L. Sommer).   20

A-10   2 7/8″   Eagle. Marked C T & O Co. Made by Vaughan, Chicago.   25

A-11   2 5/8″   A shoe marked "Drink Wooden Shoe Beer" and probably only made for the Wooden Shoe (formerly Star) Brewing Co. of Minster, Ohio.   25

A-12   2 7/8″   Sword. This type can be dated by the reported advertising on one piece: "Shrine Victory Convention, July, 1946, San Francisco/Burgermeister, A truly fine pale beer."   12-15

A-13   2 7/8″   Auto. Marked "Pat. Nov. 7, 1911. (Design Patent No. 41,895 to John L. Sommer of Newark, N.J. assigned to J.L. Sommer Mfg. Co.) This type most commonly has an advertisement for a service station, auto parts supplier, or auto dealer. Brewery advertising for Star and Schell are know.   25

A-14   2 3/4″   Bridge. Only repored marked "Rainier Beer."   25

A-15   2 7/8″   Eagle head and bottle. Bottle cap depicted at key chain hole end. Some marked "C T & O Co., Chicago, Pat. Appld. For." Others marked "Pat'd 4-30-12." Appears in 1922 Vaughan catalog with reference to the square hold as "Prest-O-Lite Key."   10-12

A-16   2 7/8″   Elk head and bottle. Crown cap at key chain hold end. Marked "C T & O Co., Chicago, Patented."   18-20

A-17   2 7/8″   Lion head and bottle.   15-17

A-18   3 1/8″   Fish. Marked "Pat. Nov. 7, 1911." (Design Patent No. 41,894 to John L. Sommer).   16-18

A-19   3 1/8″   Alligator. The slot next to the square hole is used for opening cigar boxes.   25

A-20   3 1/8″   Hand. Same shape as the A-18 fish, but depicts a hand with pointing finger marked "You pay." Reverse of opener is marked "Spin to see who wins." Knob punched in center used for spin.   16-18

A-21   3 1/4″   Hand. Spinner marked like A-20. Made by Brown & Bigelow Co., St. Paul, Minn.   8-10

A-22   2 7/8″   Bottle. Only reported for Ballantine Export Beer, New Jersey.   20

A-23   2 1/2″   Stainless steel opener made by Dow, St. Paul.   8

A-24   2 1/2″   Bottle. Crown cap at key chain hole end.   20

A-25   3″   Bottle. The "handle" portion of the opener is in the shape of a bottle (one dimension) and the top of the bottle is depicted in the lifter portion. This type and A-26/A-38 were sometimes enamelled on the bottle label. All are significantly more valuable with all original paint.   25

A-26   3 1/2″   Bottle. See A-25   25

A-27   3 1/4″   Bottle. The example shown here is from the Peter Doelger Brewery of New York and the cap lifter hook is used as a banner for Doelger's First Prize Beer.   20

A-28   3 1/4″   Bottle with square hole. Marked "Patd Mar. 12-1912." (Design Patent No. 42,305 to John L. Sommer) The cap lifter hook is often depicted as a portion of a horn type handle on a corkscrew.   12-15

A-29   3 1/4″   Bottle without square hole — see A-28.   12-15

A-30   2 3/4″   Legs with ballet slippers. Shown in 1922 Vaughan catalog as the "Dancer." With and without square hole.   22

A-31   3 3/8″   A seal marked "Get the national habit, cash in on National Oil Seals." Made for that company and does not exist with beer advertising.   —

A-32   2 1/2″   In shape of Wooden Shoe and marked "Ask for Wooden Shoe Lager Beer." (See notes on type A-11).   25

A-33   3 1/4″   Fish. Spinner. Marked "You Pay" on obverse and "Spin to see who pay" on reverse. Made by L.F. Dow Co., St. Paul, Minn.   25

A-34   3 1/8″   A fancy powderhorn.   25

A-35   (see A-7)

A-36   3″   Hand. Spinner. Corkscrew. Not reported with beer advertising.   —

A-37   3 1/2″   Hand. Type marked "Hand Brewery" made for Peter Hand Brewery of Chicago, Illinois.   25

A-38   2 3/4″   Bottle. (See notes on type A-25).   25

A-39   3″   Turtle with three screwdrivers made by Brown & Bigelow, St. Paul, Minn. Design Patent No. 161,321 was issued to Le Emmette V. de Fee on Dec. 26, 1950 and assigned to B & B. A common modern advertising piece. Uncommon with brewing company name. Example shown is from A. Gettleman Brewing Co. Value with beer advertising: 10

A-40   3 1/4″   Nude female figure wading in water. High relief brass. Marked on reverse: Copyright "1913 Braun & Co., Sept. Morn."   30

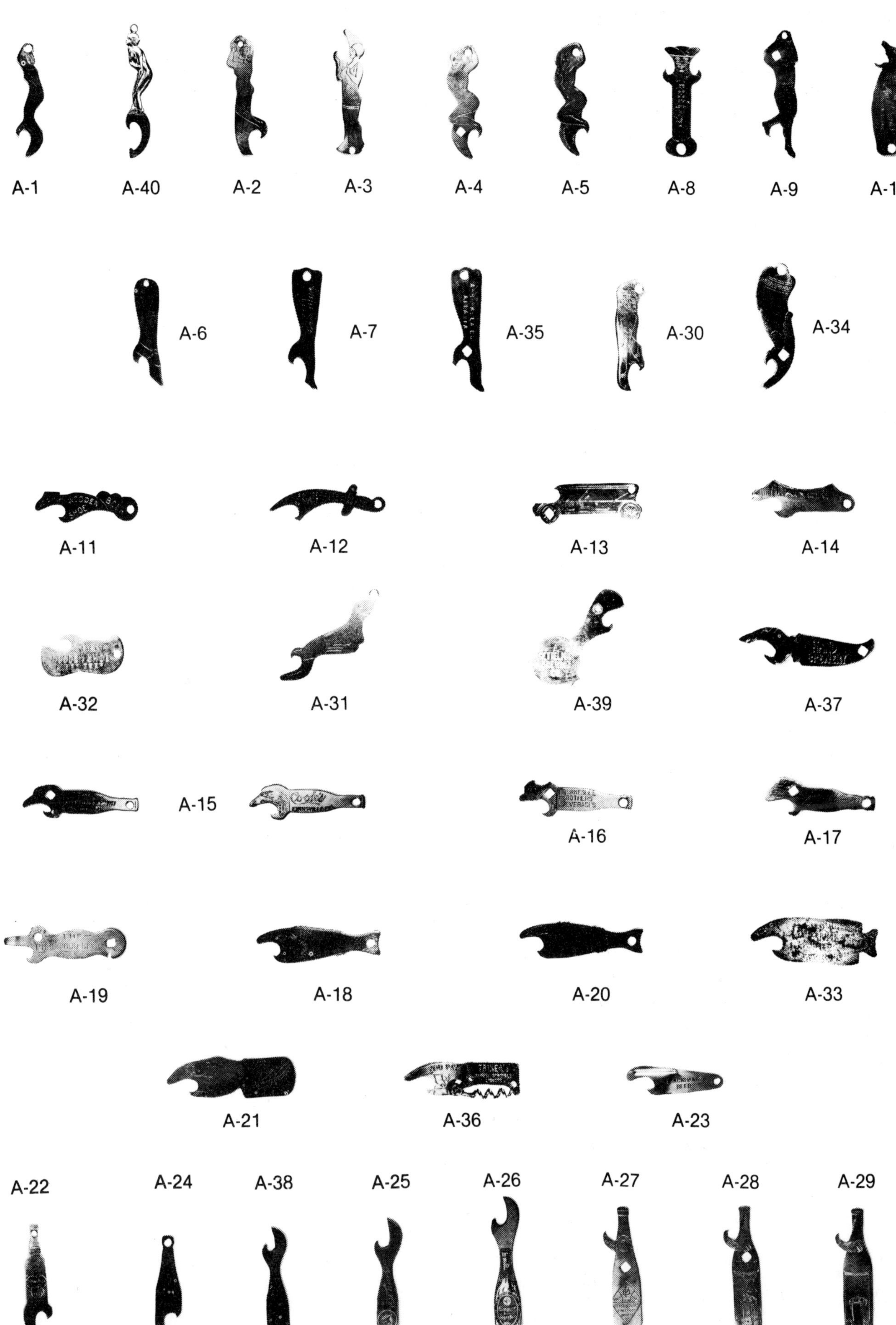

A-1
A-40
A-2
A-3
A-4
A-5
A-8
A-9
A-10
A-6
A-7
A-35
A-30
A-34
A-11
A-12
A-13
A-14
A-32
A-31
A-39
A-37
A-15
A-16
A-17
A-19
A-18
A-20
A-33
A-21
A-36
A-23
A-22
A-24
A-38
A-25
A-26
A-27
A-28
A-29

TYPE B KEY SHAPED OPENERS

B-1	2 1/2″	Usually made of brass; some made of steel and enamelled.	15-20
B-2	3 1/8″	Usually made of brass; also reported in steel and copper. The lettering is raised and the background often is in black with some red for details. Original paint increases value.	15-20
B-3	3 1/8″	Same as B-2 with cigar box opener added and key chain hole larger.	18-25
B-4	3 1/8″	Like B-2 but no square hole and key chain hold slighter larger.	15-20
B-5	3 1/8″	Steel cap lifter with cigar box nail puller. The end with round hole is split in order to slip keys on it — it serves as a key holder.	15-20
B-6	2 7/8″	Made by the W & H Co., Newark, N.J., patented Jan. 27, 1903. Tip used as screwdriver. End split as on B-5.	15-20
B-7	3 1/8″	"Handy Pocket Companion" patented Nov. 28, 1905. Opener, key holder, and button hook.	15-20
B-8	2 3/8″	Cap lifter, cigar box opener, and Prest-O-Lite key.	15-20
B-9	2 7/8″	Cap lifter, cigar box opener, and Prest-O-Lite key.	20
B-10	2 1/2″	Simple cap lifter with Prest-O-Lite key. Note that this one does not have a key chain hole. One could use the square hole but it would not serve its purpose.	16
B-11	3″	These openers from the Seattle Brewing & Malting Co. have enamel pieces of various shapes attached to them depicting totem polelike figures. They are referred to as "Potlatch" openers. The story has circulated that they were given away at an Alaskan-Yukon Exposition.	25
B-12	2 7/8″	Vaughan Novelty Co.'s "Nifty" opener with button hook. The opener was patented by Harry L. Vaughan of Chicago, Illinois. Application for patent was filed August 21, 1915 and Patent #1,207,100 was issued Dec. 5, 1916. The patent drawings show the opener with corkscrew (see B-13 below). It was also made with a screw driver.	15-18
B-13	2 7/8″	Opener with corkscrew (see B-12).	5-8
B-14	2 5/8″	Vaughan's "Special Pocket Bottle Opener." The key chain end normally depicts a crown cap on both sides.	5-8
B-15	2 1/2″	Cap lifter.	12
B-16	2 1/2″	Cap lifter with Prest-O-Lite key.	18
B-17	3″	Cap lifter with oval key chain hole. Marked "The Greenduck Co., Chicago."	16
B-18*	3″	Cap lifter with double punched key chain hole.	8-12
B-19*	3″	Cap lifter with double punched key chain hole and Prest-O-Lite key.	10-14
B-20	3″	Cap lifter with Prest-O-Lite key. The quarter moon cut-out appears on several pieces in the exact same location — reason unknown. Some believe it may be caused by interference of other openers in the stamping operation.	12-14
B-21*	3″	Cap lifter with Prest-O-Lite key.	8-12
B-22	2 7/8″	Vaughan's "Outing Key Style Pocket Bottle Opener" with Prest-O-Lite key.	12-14
B-23	2 7/8″	same as B-22 but no Prest-O-Lite key.	8-12
B-24	3 1/8″	Cap lifter invented by James Andrew Murdock of Chicago, Illinois. The patent was applied for on Nov. 9, 1934. Patent No. 2,018,083 as assigned to Vaughan Novelty Mfg. Co. was granted on Oct. 22, 1935. Mr. Murdock's objective was to add a short prong at the cap lifter by forming the metal with a 90 degree twist, thus the opener would engage at least two of the duplex ribs on the flange of a bottle cap and facilitate easy removal.	6-10
B-25	3 1/4″	Cap lifter with Prest-O-Lite key.	20-25
B-26	3 1/8″	Same as B-5 but no cigar box opener.	12-16
B-27	2 1/2″	Cap lifter. Brass.	12-16
B-28	2 7/8″	Combination cap lifter, screw driver, and cigar cutter. Made by E & D Mfg. Co. of Michigan.	25
B-29	2 7/8″	Cap lifter with Prest-O-Lite key. (See note on B-10)	18-20
B-30	2 3/4″	Cap lifter. Stamped and end formed.	15-20
B-31	3 1/4″	3/16″ thick steel cap lifter with Prest-O-Lite key.	20-25
B-32	2″	Cap lifter with two key chain holes.	18
B-33	3 1/8″	Like B-4 but larger key chain hole.	15
B-34	3″	Like B-17 but with Prest-O-Lite key.	18
B-35	2 7/8″	similar to B-13	7-9
B-36	2 7/8″	similar to B-13. Note difference in position of cap lifter.	8-10
B-37	3″	Very unusual shape for a B-type opener.	25
B-38	2 7/8″	similar to B-13 except has Prest-O-Lite key	15
B-39	3 1/4″	cap lifter.	18
B-40	2 7/8″	Opener formed liked B-30 but handle is figure of bottle.	22
B-41	2 3/4″	Larger version of B-14.	10

*Type B-18, B-19, and B-21 are sometimes marked "Picnic - Reg. U.S. Pat. Off. Trade Mark" and "Pat. Feb. 19, 1901" and may show one of the following manufacturers' names: Adv. Novelty Co., Chicago; E.M. Blumenthal & Co., Chicago; Bachrach & Co., San Francisco; Quimby Mfg. Co., Minneapolis, Minn.; A.W. Stephens Mfg. Co., Waltham or Cambridge, Mass.; Chicago Spec. Box Co.; Oscar Heyman & Co., 43 Park Place, N.Y.C.; M.C. Rosenfeld Co., Boston; Witteman Bros., New York; Hugo Cahn & Co., New York; Colson Co.; A. Magnus Sons Co., Chicago, Ill. The patent date refers to Design Patent No. 34,096 to Augustus W. Stephens of Cambridge, Mass. Application was filed Jan. 21, 1901 and the patent drawings show type B-18.

B-1

B-2   B-3   B-4   B-33

B-5   B-26   B-6   B-7

B-8

B-9   B-10   B-11   B-12

B-13   B-35   B-36   B-38

B-14   B-41   B-15   B-16   B-32

B-17   B-34   B-18   B-19

B-20   B-21   B-22   B-23

B-24   B-25   B-27   B-29

B-31   B-37   B-30   B-40

B-39   B-28

TYPE C FLAT METAL CAP LIFTERS

C-1 2 1/2" Cap lifter. Raised letters with enamelled background.   18-25

C-2 3 3/8" Cap lifter. Raised letters with enamelled background.   18-25

C-3 2 3/4 Cap lifter with Prest-O-Lite key.   16

C-4 3 1/4" Cap lifter with Prest-O-Lite key. Pabst used this style opener as a promotional piece in 1916.   5-8

C-5 3 1/4" Cap lifter.   4-6

C-6 3 1/8" Cap lifter. Note differences at top and in cap lifter between this opener and C-7.   3-5

C-7 3 1/4" Cap lifter.   4-6

C-8 2" The opener shown here is marked "Caps Off Drink Grain Belt 63-502"on obverse and "Lift Up" on reverse. The hole looks like this opener was originally connected to another implement and it swivelled into position in the fashion of types I-19 and 20 shown later in the book.   ?

C-9 3 1/8" Cap lifter.   3-5

C-10 3 1/8" Cap lifter. An opener in this style is marked "Phoenix Beer-Ale" on obverse and "Conserve steel for defense, don't lose this opener" on the reverse - one to watch for (10-15)   3-5

C-11 3 1/8" Cap lifter.   4-6

C-12 3 1/8" Cap lifter. The difference between this opener and C-13 is: On C-12 the lifter "tab" is cut partially into the base and on C-13 the lifter "tab" is confined to the open area. Some marked "Vaughan, Chicago."   2-5

C-13 3 1/8" Cap lifter. Some marked "Vaughan, Chicago."   2-5

C-14 3 1/4" Cap lifter. With and without hanger hole.   2-5

C-15 3 3/8" Cap lifter. Style produced by Handy Walden Co. The following marks have been noted: "Walden, Camb., Mass." (prob. late 50's); "Handy Walden, N.Y., U.S.A. 61" (1961); "Handy Walden, N.Y., U.S.A."; "Handy Button, N.Y.C.." This type is shown in a Feb., 1961 Handy Walden catalog and it is the only "C" type cap lifter offered in the catalog.   3-5

C-16 3 3/4" Cap lifter. Most are marked Vaughan, Chicago.   2-5

C-17 3 3/4" Cap lifter. Most are marked Vaughan, Chicago.   2-5

C-18 4 1/4" Cap lifter. Some marked "Vaughan, Made in U.S.A."   2-5

C-19 4" Cap lifter. Some are made of steel, others aluminum.   3-5

C-20 4 1/2" Cap lifter.   6-8

C-21 4 1/4" Cap lifter.   7-9

C-22 5" Cap lifter. This opener was designed by Ferdinand Neumer of New York City. Design Patent No. 91,635 was issued on Feb. 27, 1934 and assigned to the Jacob Ruppert Corp. of New York. The opener is marked "Jacob Ruppert, Brewer-New York" on the obverse and "Save this opener, Order by the case, Knickerbocker, the brew that satisfies" on the reverse. The opener style also exist with "Molson" imprinted on it. Since the patent claim was for an ornamental design and the hops, malt, and barley depicted appear on the Ruppert opener and not on the Molson there was probably no patent infringement litigation.   6

C-23 4 5/8" Thick steel cap lifter. Only Jackson Brewing Co., New Orleans, La. advertising has been reported on this opener.   15

C-24 4" Cap lifter.   10-20

C-25 3 1/2" Bottle shape cap lifter.   18

C-26 3 1/4" A cross between C-6 and C-7 with corkscrew.   16

C-27 2 7/8" Cap lifter. Cap lifter is bent up about 45 degrees from handle.   15

C-28 3 1/4" Cap lifter with Prest-O-Lite key.   5-8

C-29 3 1/4" Cap lifter with Prest-O-Lite key.   5-8

C-30 3 1/8" Unusual pre-prohibition cap lifter with Prest-O-Lite key.   25

C-31 3 1/8" Cap lifter with cigar box opener.   15

C-32 3 1/4" Cap lifter.   4-6

C-33 3 3/4" Cap lifter.   15

C-34 3 1/2" Cap lifter made by Ekco, Chicago.   8

C-1 C-2 C-3 C-4 C-5 C-28 C-29

C-6 C-7 C-26 C-8 C-9 C-10 C-11 C-31

C-30 C-12 C-13 C-14 C-15 C-32 C-27

C-16 C-17 C-33

C-18 C-19 C-20 C-34

C-21 C-22 C-23

C-24 C-25

TYPE D CAST IRON CAP LIFTERS

These cast iron openers were among the first cap lifters produced in the late 1800's when the crown cap was introduced. An opener similar to type D-6 appears in the patent drawings of Patent No. 514,200 which was issued to William Painter of Baltimore, Maryland on Feb. 6, 1894. The patent was applied for on June 5, 1893 and assigned to the Crown Cork and Seal Co. The patent claims ''a capped bottle opener consisting of a suitable handle with a cap engaging lip adapted to underlie a portion of an applied bottle sealing cap, and also having a centering gage affording gaging contact with the side of the cap adjacent to the engaging lip, and still further affording fulcrum contact for enabling bearing engagement with the upper portion or top of the cap.'' Types F-10, M-47, M-48 and M-56 are marked with this Feb. 6, 1894 Patent date.

D-1	2 7/8"	Cap lifter with wire breaker.	4-6
D-2	3"	Cap lifter with Prest-O-Lite Key.	8-10
D-3	3 3/8"	Cap lifter.	4-6
D-4	3 3/4"	Cap lifter.	4-6
D-5	3 5/8"	Cap lifter.	4-6
D-6	3 1/2"	Cap lifter with bottle stopper.	8-12
D-7	3 3/4"	Cap lifter.	4-6
D-8	4 3/4"	Cap lifter, wire breaker, cigar cutter, and tamper.	22
D-9	3 1/8"	Cap lifter.	4-6
D-10	3"	Cap lifter - unusual opening at the top.	20
D-11	3 3/8"	A very expensively made cap lifter. First the opener was cast out of iron; then the highlight area was polished smooth to a bright finish, and finally the two points at the cap lifter cup were ground to a sharp point and edge. The point was to puncture the metal cap and the lifter edge fit in the narrow crevice below the cap. This combination causes the opener to grip the cap as it is removed from the bottle.	28

TYPE E WIRE FORMED OPENERS

The earliest patent for an ''E'' type opener illustrates one similar to type E-8. It is patent #1,150,083 granted to Edwin Walker of Erie, Pennsylvania on August 17, 1915. The application was filed on Sept. 21, 1909 and divided and refiled on July 19, 1910. Walker was known well for his corkscrew patents and in this patent he was claiming a crown opener ''as a new article of manufacture, a bottle cap lifter comprising a loop bent from a wire rod, and a plurality of lips swaged from the metal of the loop and extending inwardly from the inner contour of the loop.''

E-1	3 1/2"	Cap lifter with handle flat at base.	6-10
E-2	3 1/2"	Cap lifter with handle rounded at base and cap lifter portion in tight circle.	6-10
E-3	3 1/2"	Cap lifter with handle rounded at base and squared top.	5-7
Types E-1 — E-3 sometimes called ''Wide wire hoops'' or ''Wide wire loops.''			
E-4		Single handle cap lifter in varying lengths from 4 1/4"to 4 3/4". Some have single fret (or tab) at top of hoop, two frets at base of hoop, three frets; rounded tops, flat tops, dipped tops; or screwdriver end.	4-10
E-5	4 1/4"	Bone handle cap lifter. Usually produced in two color.	7-10
E-6	3 1/2"	Cap lifter with handle flat at base and three frets at top.	7-9
E-7	3 1/2"	Cap lifter with handle flat at base and two frets at top.	7-9
E-8	3 1/8"	Early E type - smaller than more common E-10 and E-14 types; two frets at top.	7-9
E-9	3 1/4"	Another early E type. Three frets.	7-9
E-10	3 1/4"	Squared top cap lifter with two or three frets.	4-6
E-11	4 5/8"	Double stem cap lifter.	5-6
E-12	3 3/4"	Cap lifter.	3-6
E-13	3 1/2"	Cap lifter with two frets at top.	3-6
E-14	3 1/2"	The most common type wire cap lifter. Three frets at top.	1-6
E-15	4 3/4"	Unusual combination of cap lifter and paint can lid lifter (i.e. for beer advertising - this type is commonly seen with paint advertising.)	15
E-16	3 1/2"	Cap lifter with handle flat at base and single fret at top.	7-9
E-17	2 1/2"	Rarest of the E all wire type cap lifters.	17-19
E-18	3 1/2"	Like E-1 except two frets at top instead of three.	6-10
E-19	4"	Cap lifter with wooden handle in shape of bottle.	12
E-20	5 1/4"	Bone handle cap lifter. Usually produced in two color.	7-9
E-21	3 1/4"	Cap lifter with rounded handle base and two frets at top.	9
E-22	3 1/4"	Cap lifter flat at handle base, single fret at top and bent to about a 30º angle for better leverage.	8-10
E-23	3 1/4"	Cap lifter with two frets at top.	7-9
E-24	5 1/2"	Cap lifter with wooden handle.	14

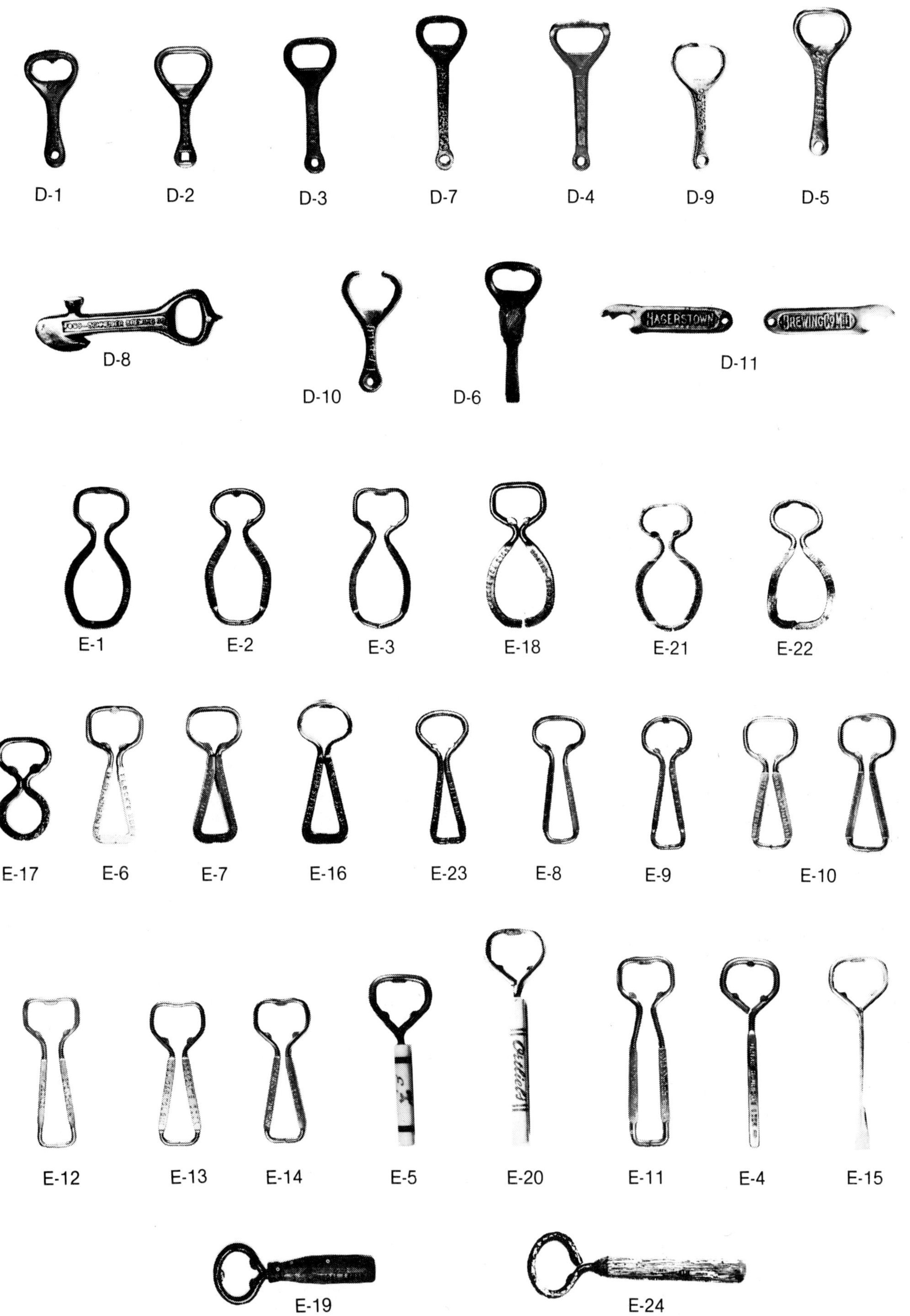
D-1
D-2
D-3
D-7
D-4
D-9
D-5
D-8
D-10
D-6
HAGERSTOWN
BREWING CO MD
D-11
E-1
E-2
E-3
E-18
E-21
E-22
E-17
E-6
E-7
E-16
E-23
E-8
E-9
E-10
E-12
E-13
E-14
E-5
E-20
E-11
E-4
E-15
E-19
E-24

TYPE F MULTI-PURPOSE OPENERS

F-1 7 7/8″ Combination cap lifter and spoon. Made by L.F. Dow. Co. 12-15

F-2 7 3/4″ Combination cap lifter and spoon. On Sept. 22, 1931 a design patent (#85,178) was issued to Thomas Harding of Newark, N.J. for an "Ornamental design for a beverage spoon or similar article, as shown." A type F-2 is shown in the patent papers. The patent was assigned to the J.L. Sommer Manufacturing Company, a Corporation of New Jersey. 12-15

F-3 8″ Combination cap lifter, can opener, and spoon. On Oct. 31, 1950 design patent #160,695 was issued to Le Emmette V. De Fee of St. Paul, Minn. as assignor to Brown & Bigelow, St. Paul, Minn., a corporation of Minnesota. The application for patent was filed Feb. 10, 1949. 10-12

F-4 7 1/4″ Combination cap lifter and spoon. Made by B & B (Brown & Bigelow), St. Paul, Minn. 10-12

F-5 7 3/4″ Combination cap lifter, cigar cutter, and pick. 16-18

F-6 6 1/4″ In a 1928 Chas. Weiland, Inc. (New York distributors of hardware supplies, etc.) catalog this item is offered as a "Four in 1 Handy Tool." It is a combination bottle opener, friction cover opener, ice pick, and milk bottle cap lifter. They were priced at 60ᶜ per dozen or $6.85 per gross. Marked Pat. 1-26-12. 7-8

F-7 7 1/4″ Combination cap lifter and ice pick. Bone handle like type E-5. 12-14

F-8 10″ Combination cap lifter and ice pick. Wooden handle. 16-18

F-9 9 1/8″ Combination cap lifter and ice pick. Heavy steel (4oz.) 25

F-10 4 1/2″ Cap lifter and (?) ice pick. This probably is type M-48 without the bone handle and was not intended as an ice pick. M-48 is not easily removed from the sleeve. The only reported advertising on F-10 and M-48 is Bullfrog Beer. Cap lifters are marked "Patd Feb.6.94" (See Patent notes under D types). 15

F-11 10 1/2″ Combination cap lifter and spatula. 30

F-12 10 1/2″ Combination cap lifter and slotted ladle. Design Patent No. 47,016 was issued Feb. 23, 1915 to John L. Sommer of Newark, N.J. for this "Kitchen Utensil." 30

F-13 11 5/8″ Combination cap lifter and cake server (Cake & Beer?!). Design Patent No. 46,702 was issued Nov. 24, 1914 to John L. Sommer and Thomas Harding of Newark, N.J. for this "Combination Bottle Opener and Cake Turner." 30

F-14 5 3/4″ Combination cap lifter, wire breaker, and ice pick. 25

F-15 7 1/2″ Combination cap lifter and spoon. Made by B & B, St. Paul. 10-12

F-16 6 1/4″ A cork puller. All steel. 20

F-17 8″ Combination cap lifter and cocktail (olive) fork. 30

F-18 8 1/4″ Combination cap lifter and ice pick. Design Patent No. 46,311 was issued Aug. 25, 1914 to Thomas Harding and assigned to J.L. Sommer Manufacturing Co. 25

F-19 8 7/8″ Combination cap lifter and ice pick. Wooden handle. 25

F-20 6 7/8″ Combination cap lifter and "branding iron." Marked "Storz" on branding iron and on handle: "Enjoy its Bitter-Free Flavor/Your Favorite Brand." Made by Vaughan, Chicago. 35

F-21 7 1/2″ Similar to F-15 except also has corkscrew. 20

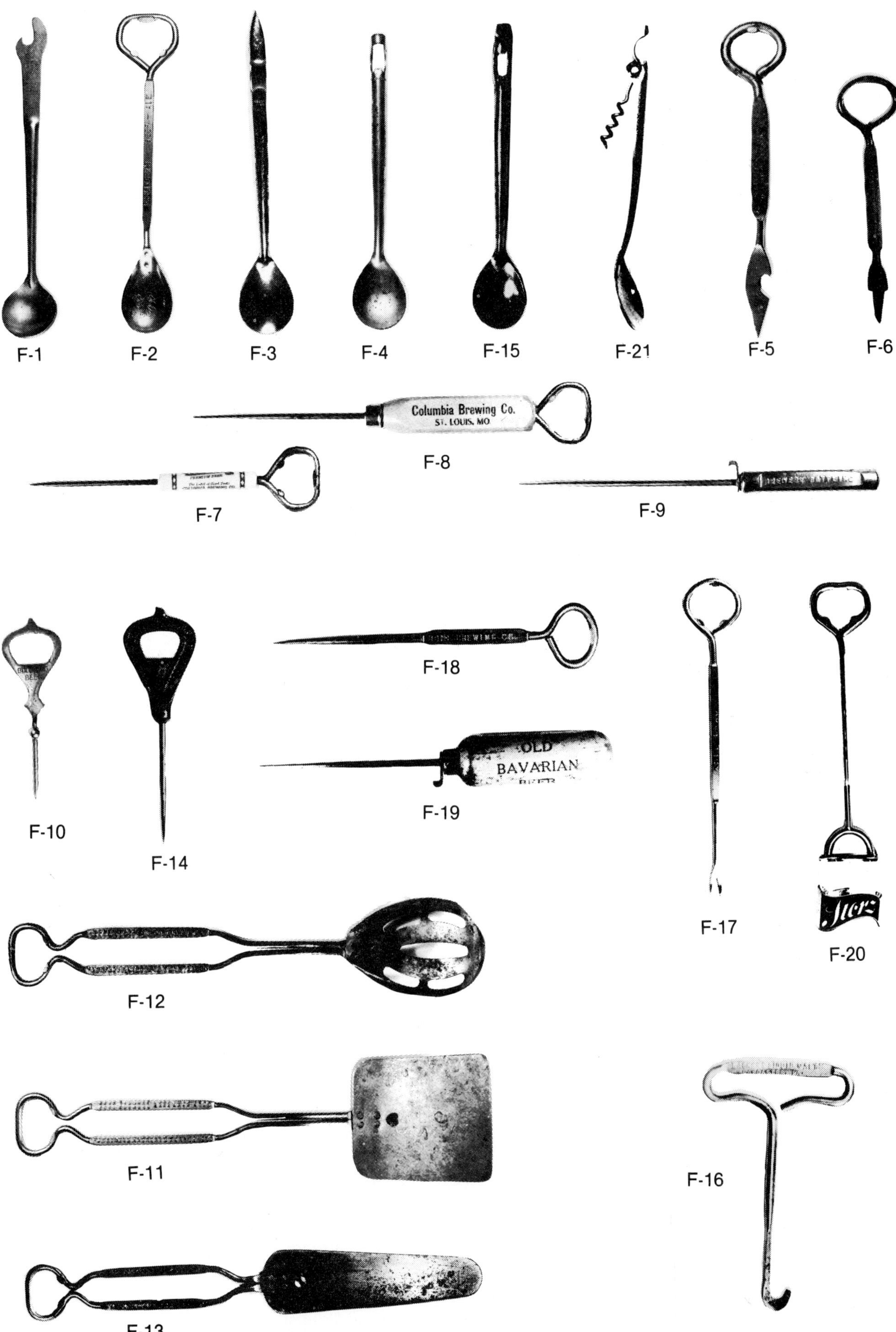

F-1
F-2
F-3
F-4
F-15
F-21
F-5
F-6
Columbia Brewing Co.
ST. LOUIS, MO
F-8
F-7
F-9
F-10
F-14
F-18
OLD
BAVARIAN
F-19
F-17
F-20
F-12
F-11
F-16
F-13

TYPE G CAP LIFTERS

G-1 4″   Formed metal cap lifter. Bottle is often depicted on handle. Made in U.S.A. by Vaughan, Chicago and in Canada by Lunn, Montreal. A Canadian example exist marked "Regd. 1935" (Black Horse Ale).   5-10

G-2 3 5/8″ Curved cap lifter.   4.6

G-3 3 5/8″ Cap lifter made by B & B, St. Paul. The cap lifter is the same as the cap lifter on the type F-4 combination cap lifter and spoon. Has also been reported with the corkscrew like type F-21. 8-10 without corkscrew. 16-18 with corkscrew.

G-4 3 1/4″ Curved cap lifter. Some are marked "Capitol Stampings Corp., Milwaukee, Wis."   6-8

G-5 3 1/4″ Similar to G-4 but flat across the handle portion. Has been noted with the following marks: 1. "Sealtite, 115 Maiden Lane, New York City, Pat'd July 13, 1909." 2. "Mf'd by Ryede Specialty Works, Patents Pending." 3. "Mf'd by Ryede Speciality Works, 137 Main St., W., Rochester, N.Y., Patented." 4. "N.Y. Specialty by 'Sesco' Pat. July 13, 1909" This opener was patented by Adolph Rydquist of Rochester, N.Y. (No. 928,156).   6-8

G-6 3″   Cap lifter with curved handle. Marked "Walden, Cambridge, Mass." and manufactured by Walden, 16 Concord Lane, Cambridge 38, Mass. as their product #108.   5-6

G-7 3″   Another Walden #108 cap lifter with flat handle instead of contoured as G-6.   5-6

G-8 4 1/8″ Cap lifter made by Vaughan, Chicago.   4-5

G-9 4 5/8″ This opener was manufactured by the Edlund Co. of Burlington, Vermont. The wood handles were imprinted with a hot foil process. They come in a variety of colors — red, yellow, green, blue, natural. Patented Nov. 7, 1933 by Henry J. Edlund of Burlington, No. 1,934,594. The application was filed Feb. 27, 1933.   4-8

G-10 4″   Cap lifter with corkscrew and bottle stopper.   20

G-11 4 3/4″ Cap lifter which looks like it belongs in a collection of tableware. The only reported beer advertising for this type is "Muessel Silver Edge." Rare.   45

G-12 1 7/8″ Lightweight metal cap lifter probably Canadian. Example says "Black Label Beer."   3-4

G-13 3 3/8″ This cap lifter is shown in a 1922 Vaughan Novelty Mfg. Co. catalog as the "Perfection" Hand Bottle Opener #50. The price was $2.00 per gross (144) and minimum quantity order for opener stamped with advertising was 50 gross. Made of nickeled steel.   4-6

G-14 3 1/8″ Advertising printed on plastic sleeve slipped over metal formed opener.   8

G-15 through G-18 are recent creations designed for resale in souvenier and novelty shops. In August of 1980 some were reported available in a Denver souvenier shop for $2.49 each.

G-19 3 1/4″ Cap lifter with bottle stopper. Marked "Mf'd by Ryede Specialty Works, Patents Pending."   20

G-20 3 3/4″ Recent cap lifter made by Century, Canada. Copper colored.   5

G-21 4 3/8″ Cap lifter contoured like bottle.   10

G-22 4 1/4″ Cap lifter similar to G-8 but longer and narrower.   5-6

TYPE H OVER THE TOP STYLE CAP LIFTERS

On April 15, 1924 Harry L. Vaughan of Chicago, Illinois was granted Patent No. 1,490,149 for the invention of the over the top style opener (Type H-1, 2, 3). The opener is formed by stamping out of a strip of metal a blank of proper conformation and then bending it into final form by means of suitable dies. The patent application was filed on Dec. 1, 1921 and was assigned to the Vaughan Novelty Mfg. Co. The opener is shown in the 1922 Vaughan catalog as product No. 104 with the following comments: "A slight downward pressure and off comes the cap in the hand. Everybody says - The best Bottle Opener ever invented." Prices ranged from $7.50 for 250 to $17.00 per thousand in 10,000 quantity.

H-1 3 1/2″ Cap remover with widening contoured handle.   6-8

H-2 3 3/8″ Cap remover - some made by Vaughan, Chicago and others made by G.G. Greene Co., Warren, Pa. A sideview of the Vaughan opener shows a pair of curvilinear bearing edges which engage the top surface of the bottle cap; The Greene opener has these edges coming to a point.   4-6

H-3 4 1/4″ Made by Vaughan and Greene as H-2.   5-7

H-4 3 3/4″ Over the top style cap lifter with folding corkscrew. Marked "Patented Dec. 11, 28 JEMCO (in diamond), Feb. 12, 29, The J.E. Mergott Co., Newark, N. J." Patent #1,695,098 to C. Hiering of Newark, N.J.   18

H-5 4″   Cap lifter used in over the top position or in conventional lifting position.   4-6

H-6 4 1/4″ Cap remover made by Vaughan, Chicago.   5-6

H-7 4 1/8″ Over the top cap remover.   6-8

H-8 4 1/8″ Lithographed over the top opener in bottle shape. All are imprinted to represent the bottle of the product advertised. The cap remover is at the top of the bottle except a Pabst which has remover at the bottom. On the reverse the Pabst is marked "Pabst Brewing Co., Milwaukee, Wis., Pat. Pend. Display 1462." Other brands are marked "Muth, Buffalo, N.Y., Copyright 1940, Pat. Pending." This type of opener is easily damaged (scratched) and conditions vary widely. Pabst, Duquesne, and Esslinger are the most common and in very good condition worth 3-4. Others in very good condition are 15-20.

H-9 3 5/8″ Very unusual over the top style opener. One reported example is marked "Schlitz & Barmann Beer / J.J. Cuneo, Kingston, N.Y."   16

H-10 3 1/2″ Like H-1 but has folding corkscrew.   15

H-11 4 1/8″ Like H-7 but single dimple instead of double.   6-8

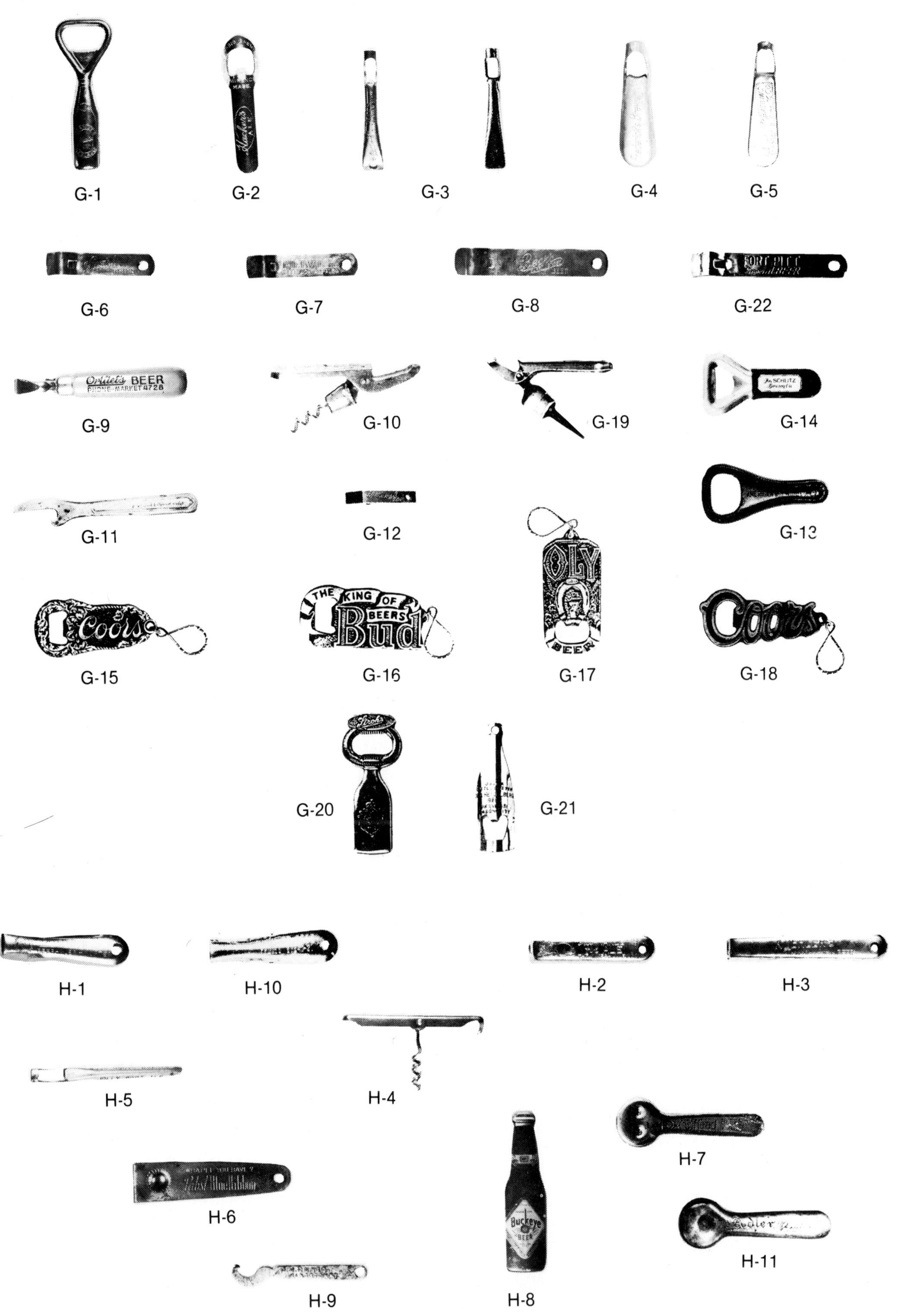

G-1   G-2   G-3   G-4   G-5

G-6   G-7   G-8   G-22

G-9   G-10   G-19   G-14

G-11   G-12   G-13

G-15   G-16   G-17   G-18

G-20   G-21

H-1   H-10   H-2   H-3

H-5   H-4

H-7

H-6

H-8

H-11

H-9

TYPE I COMBINATION CAP LIFTER/CAN PIERCER

A close inspection of any large collection of I and J type openers will reveal a vast number of variations too numerous and, no doubt, too confusing to present here. The openers shown here give the reader the basic sizes and shapes known. Variations include: slight differences in length and width; presence of "ears" designed to prevent dropping opener into bottle; bottle and can ends in opposite planes; presence or absence of hanger hole; and presence or absence of strengthening ribs. In addition to the physical variations of these openers, the presence or absence of manufacturer's names, manufacturing dates, and/or patent dates/numbers may be noted. The openers may also be copper, nickel, cadmium, chromate or brass plated. Plated openers are valued at 25% more.

I-1	3 1/4" Cap lifter/Can piercer.	6-8
I-2	4"x5/8" Cap lifter/Can piercer.	3-4
I-3	4"x3/4" Cap lifter/Can piercer.	3-4
I-4	4 1/8" Cap lifter/Can piercer designed by Michael J. LaForte of Park Ridge, Illinois. Design patent No. 143,327 was issued Dec. 25, 1945 and assigned to Vaughan Novelty Mfg. Co. The ribs were the crux of LaForte's new "ornamental" design.	3-4
I-5	4 1/4" Cap lifter/Can piercer.	2-4
I-6	4 5/8" Cap lifter/Can piercer.	2-4
I-7	4 3/4" Cap lfiter/Can piercer which was developed and patented by personnel of the American Can Company's Research Department at Maywood, Illinois. The first model was devised on August 15, 1932, with the patent applied for on April 13, 1933, and then granted on April 2, 1935 (#1,996,550)	4-6
I-8	4 1/4" Cap lifter/Can piercer.	10-12
I-9	4 5/8" Cast iron cap lifter/Can piercer.	8-10
I-10	5" Cap lifter and piercer made by Soss Manufacturing Company, Roselle, New Jersey. Patent #2,019,099 was issued to Francis H. Schwartz as assigned to Soss on Oct. 29, 1935.	10-12
I-11	3 1/4" - 3 3/8" Cap lifter/Can piercer.	1-3
I-12	3 5/8" - 3 3/4" Cap lifter/Can piercer.	1-3
I-13	3 7/8" - 4 1/8" Cap lifter/Can piercer.	1-3
I-14	4 1/4" - 4 3/8" Cap lifter/Can piercer.	1-3
I-15	4 3/4" Cap lifter/Can piercer.	2-5
I-16	3 7/8" - 4" Ribbed Cap lifter/Can piercer.	3-4
I-17	4 1/4" - 4 3/8" Ribber Cap lifter/Can piercer.	1-4
I-18	4 3/4" Ribbed cap lifter/Can piercer.	4-5
I-19	3 1/2" (open) "Quad-Fold" Cap lifter/Can piercer made by Vaughan, Chicago.	4-5
I-20	3 7/8" (open) "Quad-Fold" by Vaughan.	4-5
I-21	5" Cap lifter and Can piercer on same end. Formed metal known as the Tu-Way opener.	8
I-22	4 3/4" "Easi-Ope" can and bottle opener made by H.R. Ranson Co. of Detroit, Michigan. Patent #2,517,442 was assigned to Harland R. Ransom on Aug. 1, 1950 for this opener. Among other claims in the patent application, was a unique shape designed to prevent the contents of the can from shooting or splashing out when the can is opened.	4-6
I-23	3 3/4" Same as I-22 except no bottle cap lifter.	6-8
I-24	4 3/8" Cap lifter/Can piercer marked "PorEzy Patd."	10-12
I-25	5" Cap lifter/Can piercer for which Bernard E. Dougherty of Seattle, Wash. was granted patent No. 2,002,173 on May 21, 1935. This opener is made in two pieces. - it has a movable member inserted into the can piercer and the tooth on this member is designed to grip the flange of any can close to the edge to ensure piercing the can as close to the inside edge as possible to maximize easy removal of contents.	16
I-26	3 3/4" Cap lifter/Can piercer made by Campello, Mass.	6

TYPE J CAN PIERCERS

J-1	3 1/8" Can piercer manufactured by Walden, Cambridge, Mass.	6-8
J-2	4 1/8" x 5/8" Can piercer	3-4
J-3	4 1/8" x 3/4" Can piercer	2-4
J-4	4 3/8" Can piercer	2-4
J-5	4" Can piercer manufactured by Vaughan, Chicago, Ill.	2-5
J-6	4" Can piercer manufactured by Vaughan, marked "Pat. 143,327; 1,996,550, Others Pending, Vaughan, Chicago, Made in U.S.A." (See I-4 and I-7 for notes on these patents).	3-5
J-7	4 3/8" This folding can piercer has been reported with Coors and Hamms advertising. It is marked: "For Beer, CANCO (in oval), Patent 1,996,550." Dewitt F. Sampson of Elmhurst, Illinois and John M. Hothersall of Brooklyn, N.Y. were the individuals granted that patent with the aforesaid patent number, it is actually a later patent by Hothersall (#2,188,352 applied for on 8/6/37 and granted on 1/30/40) in which his principal objective was to improve upon the earlier design by making a foldable opener.	10
J-8	4 1/4" Can piercer *and* bottle opener. George R. Harrah filed for patent on this opener on April 5, 1950 and over 6 years later on Dec. 11, 1956 patent #2,773,272 was granted. One of the earliest pieces Mr. Harrah produced was for Ballantine and bears the mark: "Harrah, U.S.A. Pat. 1,996,550 Others Pend." Others are marked "Pat. Pend." and were obviously produced in the early 1950's. Mr. Harrah later entered in to a royalty agreement with Scovill Mfg. of Waterbury, Conn. and soon after Scovill began to produce them the market began to fall off due to the introduction of twist off caps and pull tabs.	5-8
J-9	4" This can piercer was designed by Joseph G. Pessina of St. Louis, Mo., and design patent #155,314 was issued to him on Sept. 20, 1949.	7-8
J-10	4 3/4" This can piercer is like type I-7 except it has no cap lifter. The reverse is marked: 'For beer in cans marked Keglined, trade mark Am. Can. Co., Canco, Patent 1,996,550." It has been reported only with advertising for Pabst.	12

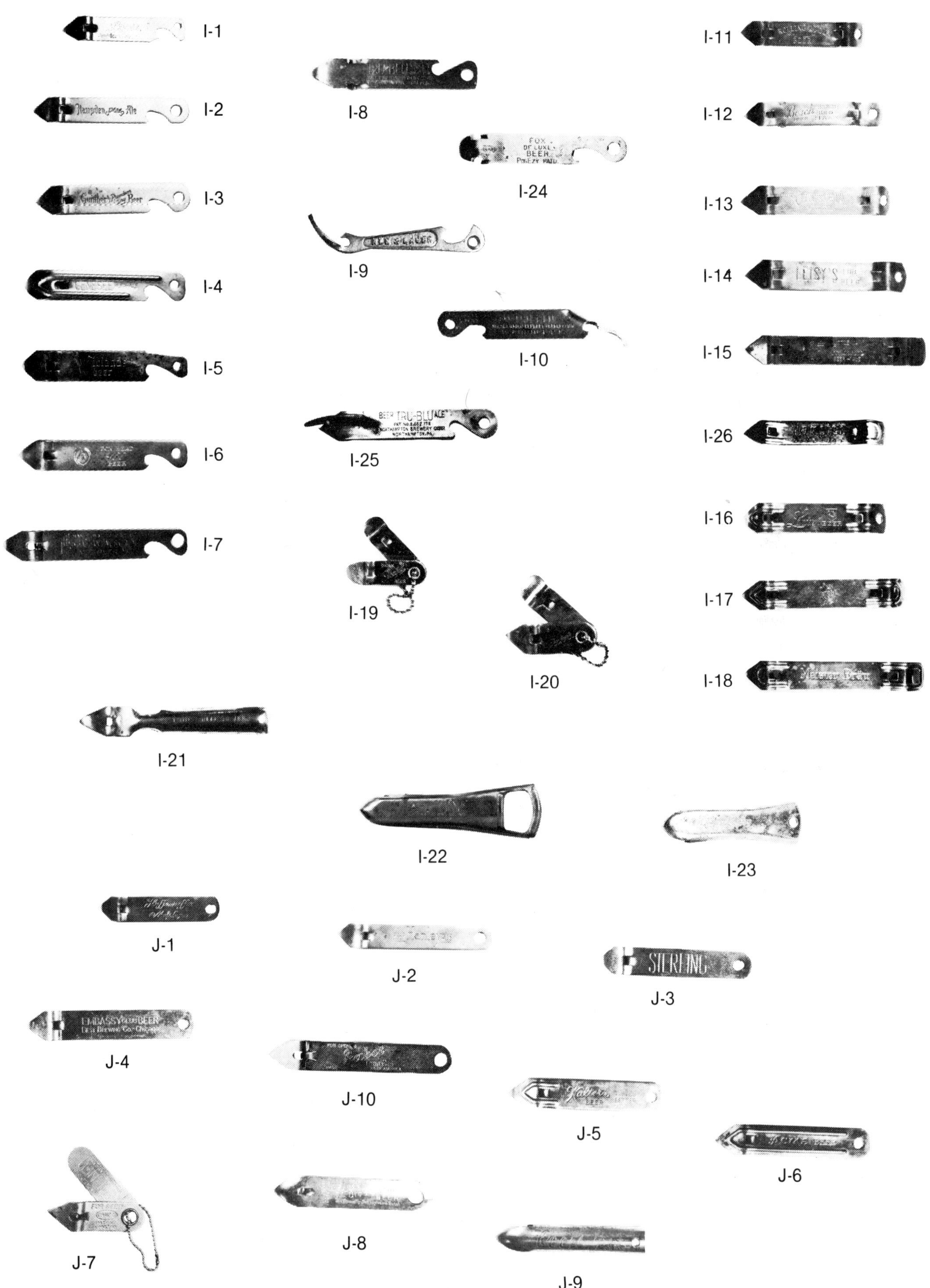

I-1
I-2
I-3
I-4
I-5
I-6
I-7
I-8
I-24
I-9
I-10
I-25
I-19
I-20
I-21
I-11
I-12
I-13
I-14
I-15
I-26
I-16
I-17
I-18
I-22
I-23
J-1
J-2
J-3
J-4
J-10
J-5
J-6
J-7
J-8
J-9

TYPE K SPECIAL CAN PIERCERS

K-1   7 3/4 " high. Heavy cast iron opener. Insert 7, 11, 12, or 16 oz. can, lower handle, and can is double pierced.   30

K-2   5 7/8 " high. Pot metal opener for 12 oz. cans. Holes in base for mounting to bar.   30

K-3   5 "   Combination can piercer and handle by Handy Walden Co. Fits 12 oz can. The "Can handle" was manufactured in 1960 for the Rheingold Brewing Company by the Handy Walden Co. The order called for one half million at a cost of 8 cents each. The production run was made and samples were distributed. In a very short time the police department realized the danger of the can handle as a weapon and asked the Handy Walden Co. to discontinue its manufacture. According to Elliot Baritz of Handy Walden almost one half million of the openers were poured into the foundation of one of Rheingold's construction projects.   16

K-4   5 3/8 " high. The "Tapster." Open lid, insert can, close lid (it pierces can), and pour. This "opener" was manufactured by Revere Copper and Brass of Rome, New York 1936-1941. It is not uncommon to find these without advertising (value 20). The "Tapster" was made with advertising for Pabst. The word Pabst appears in raised letters on both sides. One style has a square bend in the handle and a copper plated body. A second style has a chrome plated body and the handle is rounded. Supposedly there were only nine "Pabst Tapsters" made and there were none made with other advertising.   "Pabst Tapster": 250

K-5   6 "   high. Can piercer for 12 oz cans. Manufactured in cast iron by Vaughan, Chicago and in cast aluminum by Andy Wadoz & Co., Milwaukee, Wis.   25

K-6   7 3/4 " high. Unusual counter top can piercer. Can rests on platform which swings up to punch can.   50

TYPE L CAN AND BOTTLE SHAPED OPENERS

L-1   1 3/4 " high. Retractable can piercer made in West Germany in the late 1950's. Can piercer is released by pushing button on top.   8-12

L-2   2 3/4 " high mini bottle with corkscrew inside. Some are marked "Pat. Apld For" on base; others are marked "Williamson Co., Newark, N.J." with and without the patent date June 1, 1897 (Williamson Patent #583,561). The upper half unscrews from the base and the corkscrew is pulled out from the base, turned 90^0 and engaged in a slot; the top can then be screwed back on and the bottle then serves as the handle. In some of the tops there is a peephole or viewer with a magnifier. When the top is removed and held up to the light, a picture can be seen. Those marked Anheuser Busch are the most common and are valued at 18-22; Those complete with viewer and picture intact 80-100; and others 50-80.

L-3   6 " high cap lifter. Michelob bottle of wood and metal - an Anheuser-Busch promotional opener of the 1960's. Sold at that time for 84ᶜ each.   10

L-4   3 1/2 " - 4 1/4 ". Wooden mini bottle with metal cap and cap lifter attached. These were in their hey-day as advertising give-aways and as a souvenier shop item in the late 30's and 40's.   12-30

L-5   3 3/4 " Wood mini bottle with cap lifter attached.   10

L-6   2 3/4 " high mini bottle with corkscrew inside. Similar to L-2 - note square shouldered bottle.   50-100

K-1

K-5

K-2

K-3

K-6

K-4

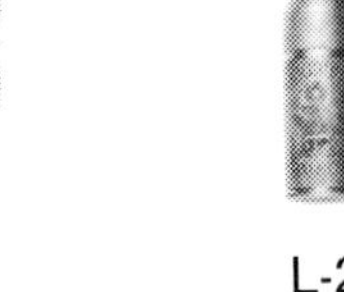

L-1

L-2

L-6

L-3

L-4

L-5

TYPE M MISCELLANEOUS OPENERS

M-1 3 1/2″ Lithographed cap lifter made by H.D. Beach Co. of Coshocton, Ohio. Some are marked with the patent date Sept. 11, 1911. Those with a picture of a bottle are valued at 25-35; others 10-20.

M-2 3 1/4″ Lithographed cap lifter - see M-1. 25-35

M-3 2 1/2″ closed. 3 1/4″ to 3 1/2″ open. Retractable or slide out opener. There are two variations of this opener: an under-and-lift style and an over the top style. The opener is steel and the casing is plated and painted over brass. Colorful openers in red, blue, black, red, green, and yellow. There are some rare beer advertising openers in this type: Flock's F and S, Bismarck, Heurich, Ruppert's and Victor. These are valued at 50-80. Others are 20-40.

M-4 3 7/8″ Flat steel opener with cap lifter punched and pressed downward in two 90° bends to grip cap. Reported only for Blatz Beer. 6

M-5 6 1/2″ Combination cap lifter and screw driver. 15

M-6 3 1/8″ Combination cap lifter and bell. Marked "Pat. Pending." 20-25

M-7 4 1/8″ Flat steel cap lifter. Top portion depicts a top. Made for Duquesne Brewing Co. of Pittsburgh, Pa. advertising Silver Top Beer, Old Nut Brown Ale, and Duquesne Pilsener. 30

M-8 3 1/4″ Steel cap lifter, handle bent at angle. Has reinforcing rib. Reported only marked "Stoney's Beer." 22

M-9 5″ Combination cap lifter and can piercer made by Vaughan Co. Reported only with advertising for Ballantine Beer on green plastic handle. 15

M-10 4″ Cap lifter in form of hand made by Vaughan for Ballantine and marked "Handy Way to Order Ballantine's" 12

M-11, M-12, and M-13. Cap lifters made for Ballantine and depicting Ballantine's famous three ring symbol marked "Purity, Body, Flavor." 8-10

M-14 6 1/8″ Combination cap lifter/can piercer produced in Germany and purchased in 1963 as a gift for persons on tour through the Schmidt's Philadelphia plant. 10

M-15 5 3/8″ Cast iron cap lifter/can piercer. Produced by Federal Die Casting Company of Chicago in 1955 for the 100th anniversery of Miller Brewing. Federal made about 2000 of this opener with brass plating for Miller and about 2000 with chrome plating and the Federal name. 25

M-16 5 3/8″ Cap lifter marked "Budweiser/Beechwood." The handles of the openers were made from old Budweiser aging tanks and the openers were given to Anheuser-Busch executives at a special company meeting. 20

M-17 5″ The Budweiser "Bow-tie" opener. Red and white on steel - made in Japan. See type N-15 for similar style. 10

M-18 6 1/2″ Cap lifter and can piercer marked "Honorary Budweiser Brewmaster, 7 Golden Keys." The Golden key was an advertising-promotional item during the 1950's. The seven keys referred to various aspects of Budweiser. 18

M-19 5 1/4″ Combination bottle opener and muddler. Frank E. Hamilton or Milwaukee, Wis. Designed this opener and on Feb. 3, 1948 was granted Design Patent No. 148,535. 15-20

M-20 6″ Pre-prohibition cap lifter marked "The Gutsch Brewing Co." (Sheboygan, Wis.). Wood handle. 22

M-21 Various lengths and shapes of bone handles with cap lifter. The collar is marked "Rainier" and "Sterling" 25

M-22 5 3/8″ Cap lifter. 15

M-23 5 1/4″ Combination can piercer, cap lifter, and folding corkscrew made by Ekco, Chicago. Plastic Handle. 10

M-24 2 1/8″ Opener marked "Coors" for push tab cans. 4

M-25 2 7/8″ Corkscrew inside bullet shape. See notes on type L-2. 25

M-26 3 1/4″ Pocket corkscrew in metal sleeve

M-27 2 7/8″ diameter. This Lone Star opener is featured in a 1975 brochure from the David Bortner Co. of Janesville, Wisconsin. Works as a spinner for deciding who pays—top point is marked "You Pay" on back. It was sold as an opener or as a combination opener key chain, belt buckle, or bolo tie. 3

M-28 4 1/4″ (opener - unfolded). Folding combination cap lifter/can piercer. Shown with original case. 15

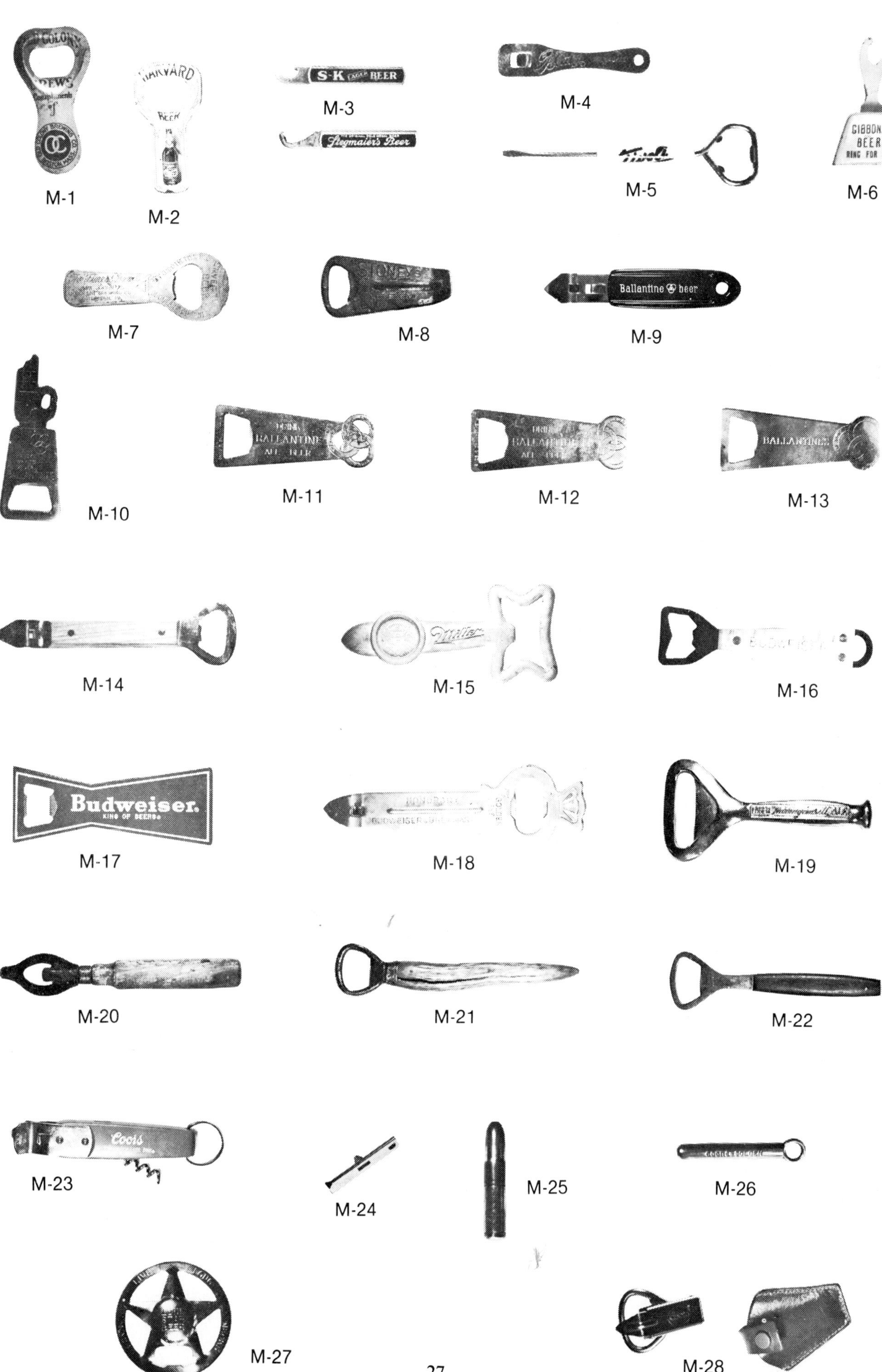

M-1
M-2
M-3
M-4
M-5
M-6
M-7
M-8
M-9
M-10
M-11
M-12
M-13
M-14
M-15
M-16
M-17
M-18
M-19
M-20
M-21
M-22
M-23
M-24
M-25
M-26
M-27
M-28

TYPE M MISCELLANEOUS OPENERS (cont.)

M-29 5 5/8″ Combination cap lifter/can piercer with plastic handle. This was developed by Mr. Lipic of St. Louis, Missouri in the early 50's and the type has met with lasting success. They are a commonly used advertising piece for all types of businesses, yet few have been reported with beer advertising. 6-8

M-30 5 3/4″ Same as above except handle end comes to a point. 6-8

M-31 5 1/2″ Can piercer with plastic handle. Bottom of handle is formed to fit finger grip. 7

M-32 4 3/4″ Combination over the top cap lifter/can piercer with plastic handles marked "Pat. App. 211,085, Nu Pro Corp." (This would be a patent application of the late 30's). The cap lifter is like type H-6. 14

M-33 6″ Combination cap lifter/can piercer with wood handle. 12

M-34 5 5/8″ Combination cap lifter, screw driver, and lid lifter with adv. imprint on plastic sleeve. Opener is marked "Alexander Husky, U.S.A. and has been a product of Alexander Manufacturing Company of St. Louis, Missouri since approximately 1975. 4

M-35 10″ This opener has only been reported with advertising for Storz Beer. It comes in a box marked "Nite Club" and inside there is a paper stating: "The Storz Nite Club Opener is a valuable accessory for your bar or kitchen. 24-Carat Gold plated. Beer Can opener, Bottle opener, Jar top lifter, Cracks ice cubes, Mixed drink muddler, Crushes sugar cubes." 35

M-36 5 1/2″ Cap lifter with wood handle. 16

M-37 4 5/8″ high. Combination opener/bell. Brass. Marked inside "Bells of Sarna Regd U.S. 230 India." 15

M-38 5 3/4″ Combination cap lifter/can piercer with adv. on plastic handle. 15

M-39 4 3/4″ Combination cap lifter/can piercer and corkscrew made by Vaughan Company, Chicago. It is a combination of G-8 (on top) and J-4 (on bottom) with a plastic spacer and corkscrew sandwiched in between. 15

M-40 5 3/4″ Combination can piercer/cap lifter. Plastic handle. Has only been reported with mark "Celebrating Our 90th Birthday 1866-1956, Oshkosh Brewing Co." and is obviously vintage 1956. 18

M-41 3 1/8″ Cap lifter with metal sleeve. 16

M-42 4 1/4″ Cap lifter with plastic barrel. 15

M-43 3 3/8″ Luggage tag style cap lifter - made in Denmark. 10

M-44 4 1/4″ Cap lifter with jar lid remover. 15

M-45 5 1/4″ Cast iron cap lifter. 18

M-46 5 3/4″ Cap lifter/can piercer with adv. on plastic sleeve. 15

M-47 5 5/8″ Cap lifter with ornate cast iron handle. Pat'd Feb 6 '94. Note: same date on this one and similar cap lifter to types F-10, M-48, and M-56. (See patent notes under D Types). 25

M-48 6 1/2″ Cap lifter with bone handle. Marked Pat. Feb. 6 '94. See F-10 20

M-49 3 - 3 1/2″ Retractable (or slide out) cap lifter with plastic handle. 8

M-50 7 1/4″ Cap lifter/can piercer. Plastic handle. Note similarity to type M-35. 15

M-51 5″ Cap lifter with plastic handle. 15

M-52 6 1/4″ Cap lifter with bone handle. Collar is marked "Sterling." 25

M-53 5 5/8″ Cap lifter, can piercer, and corkscrew. Plastic handles. Made by Colonial Knife Co., Providence, Rhode Island. 2-4

M-54 5 5/8″ Same as above but no corkscrew. Shown in 1980 Stroh's Brewery (Detroit) gift shop catalog at $1.75.

M-55 9 1/2″ Combination tap knob handle and can piercer/cap lifter from International Breweries, Buffalo, N.Y. and Frankenmuth, Mich. This was a presentation piece for beer wholesalers. 20

M-56 6″ Cap lifter. See notes on M-48. The opener shown here is marked "Pfaff's Lager, 1857-1907." 25

M-57 5 7/8″ Cast iron cap lifter with wooden handle. 18

M-58 6 3/4″ Brass plated cast iron opener. 20

M-59 5″ An opener. Incorrectly reported in Just for Openers as a beer advertising opener. The Miller logo on the opener shown is for Miller Fluid Power Co. in Bensenville, Illinois.

M-60 3 1/4″ Cap lifter with plastic handle. 8-10

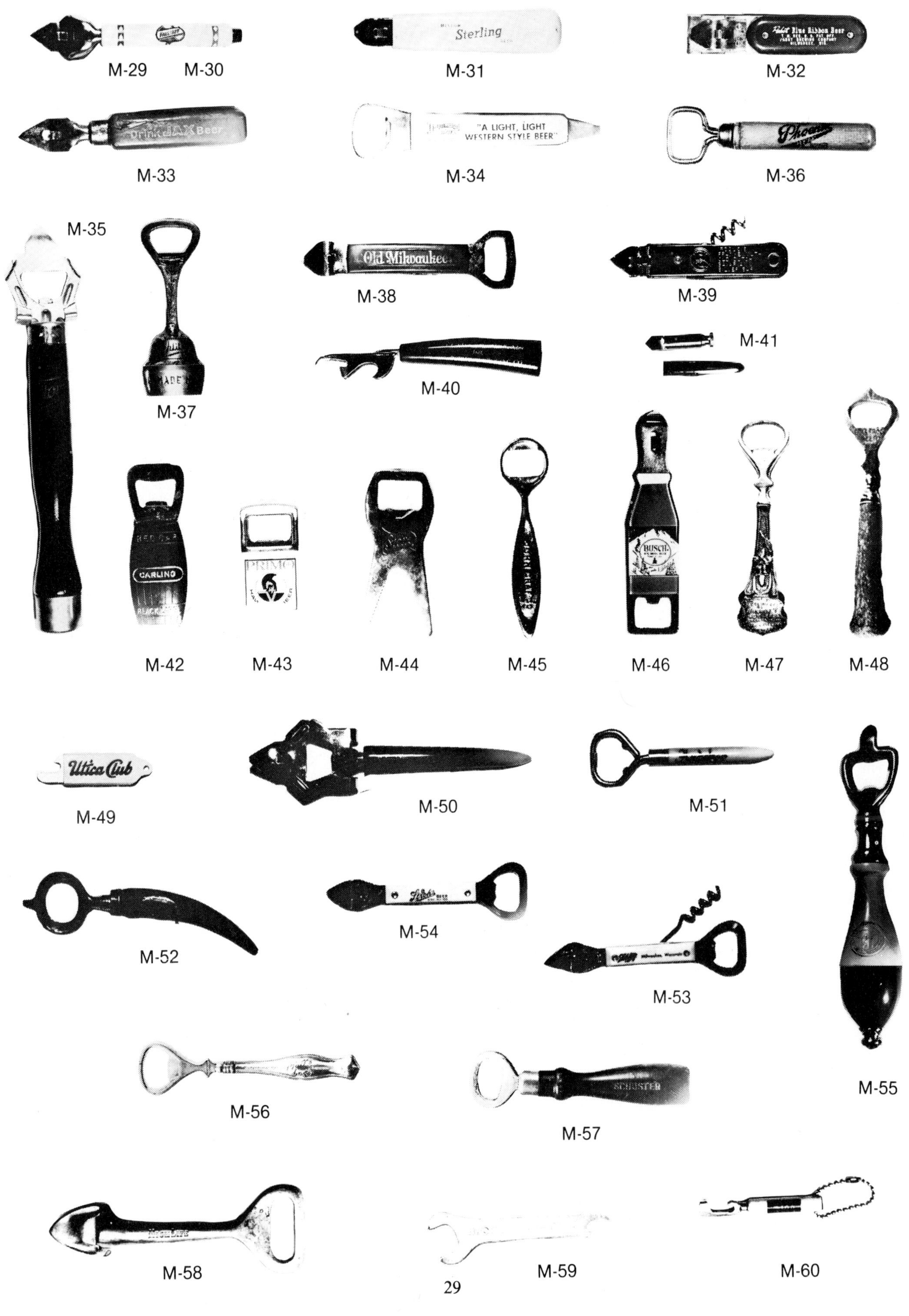

M-29   M-30
M-31
M-32
Sterling
Pabst Blue Ribbon Beer
M-33
Drink JAX Beer
M-34
"A LIGHT, LIGHT WESTERN STYLE BEER"
M-36
Phoenix
M-35
M-37
M-38
Old Milwaukee
M-39
M-40
M-41
M-42
CARLING
RED CAP
M-43
PRIMO
M-44
M-45
M-46
BUSCH
M-47
M-48
M-49
Utica Club
M-50
M-51
M-52
M-54
Stroh's BEER
M-53
M-55
M-56
M-57
SCHUSTER
M-58
M-59
M-60

TYPE N NOVELTY OPENERS

N-1 3″ Combination cap lifter and screw driver (inside). Vintage 1939. 15

N-2 2 1/2″ Cap lifter with handle in shape of a bowling pin. 4

N-3 2 1/4″ Single blade knife/opener marked "Bassett U.S.A. Patd, 2,779,098. This opener is shown in the Bassett "Kustom King" catalog of January, 1980 dubbed the "Derby Duke." Prices range from 53ᶜ each in quantities of 240-499 and 36ᶜ each in quantities of 10,000 and up.

N-4 3″ Opener with single knife blade. Blade marked "Etched P. Co., L.I.C. (Long Island City), N.Y." 18

N-5 3 1/4″ Opener with two knife blades in shape of lady's leg. Marked "Utica Cutlery, Utica, N.Y." Ivory handles. has only been reported with advertising for the West End Brewing Company of Utica. 55

N-6 3 1/4″ From Griffon Cutlery Works, Germany a bottle shaped combination tool - cap lifter, corkscrew, cigar cutter, file, and knife. 50

N-7 3″ Cap lifter with sliding cigar cutter and Prest-O-Lite Key. Marked Pat. 10.12.09. 30

N-8 3 3/8″ Cap lifter with sliding cigar cutter, cigar box opener, Prest-O-Lite Key, and screwdriver. Marked Pat. 10.12.09. The inventor was John L. Sommer of Newark, N.J.—Patent No. 936,678. 30

N-9 3 1/8″ Cap lifter and bottle cap resealer made by Vaughan, Chicago.

N-10 3 1/8″ Cap lifter and bottle stopper marked "Pat'd U.S.A. Dec. 9, 19, Nos. 1,324,256." The patent was only for the bottle stopper and was issued to William B. Langan of Hawley, Pennsylvania and assigned to Koscherak Siphon Bottle Works of Hoboken, New Jersey. 18

N-11 3 3/8″ Cap lifter and shoe horn. This type is shown in a 1961 Handy Walden catalog as their product #1048. In a 1971 Vaughan catalog another combination shoe horn and bottle opener of slightly different design is shown. Those that have been reported with beer advertising were made by Handy Walden. 12

N-12 6 1/2″ Cap lifter and lighter (round end cap removes to expose lighter). The lighter portion is marked "Redilite, Pat. 1,820,131, Made in U.S.A., B. & B., St. Paul, Minn." The patent number refers to the lighter and was issued to Howard L. Fischer of St. Paul on Aug. 25, 1931. 20

N-13 12″ Cap lifter and can piercer on miniature wood baseball bat. Reported only marked "Baseball and Ballantine Beer." 25

N-14 3 5/8″ Folding combination cap lifter and bottle seal. Patent #2,179,158 was granted to P.J. Marks of Rochester, New York on Nov. 7, 1939. It is marked "Topper" which is the manufacturer's trade name and not a beer. The opener probably does not exist with beer advertising.

N-15 2 5/8″ Budweiser "Bow-tie" made in Japan. Two knife blades - one with cap lifter. See type M-17 for similar style. 12

N-16 3 1/2″ Cast iron miniature cannon with cap lifter marked "Valley Forge." This is probably a souvenier of Valley Forge and not advertising for the beer of that name.

N-17 9 1/2″ Cap lifter and can piercer on wood belaying pin marked "Have a taste of pleasant living . . . have a National Beer!" Approximately 100,000 of these openers were sold between 1960 and 1963. It was designed by John Schneider of National Brewing Co. A belaying pin was used on the Clipper Ships to hang and release ships' lines and ropes. The cap lifter/can piercer is the same as types N-13 and M-33. 25

N-18 2 3/8″ Combination cap lifter and screwdriver on one blade; other two blades are knife and file. 5

N-19 6 1/2″ Combination cap lifter, corkscrew (attached to lifter and inserted in handle), jigger, ice cracker, and drink recipe viewer. A sleeve over the handle turns to expose different recipes through openings. 8

N-20 3″ Shown in Vaughan Co.'s 1922 catalog as the "Jim Dandy" 4 in Pocket Tool: Bottle opener, button hook, cigar cutter, and screwdriver. Prices ranged from $20.00 for 500 to $27.50 per thousand in 10,000 lots. 25

N-21 5 1/2″ An opener for malt cans. 10

N-22 7″ Combination cap lifter and pencil. 25

N-23 3″ Eighteen wheel truck with opener/screwdriver blade and single knife blade. Made by Colonial Knife Co. of Providence, Rhode Island. Shown in their Feb. 1980 Ambassador Line catalog at prices ranging from $6.25 ea. for 100 to $4.90 for 2000.

N-24 3″ Cap lifter with single knife blade. Blade marked "Stainless, Sheffield, England." 20

N-25 3 1/4″ Cap lifter with single knife blade in handle. 5

N-26 5 1/2″ Combination cap lifter, lid pry, and jar top opener. These are quite common with advertising other than beer. With beer adv. rare. 25

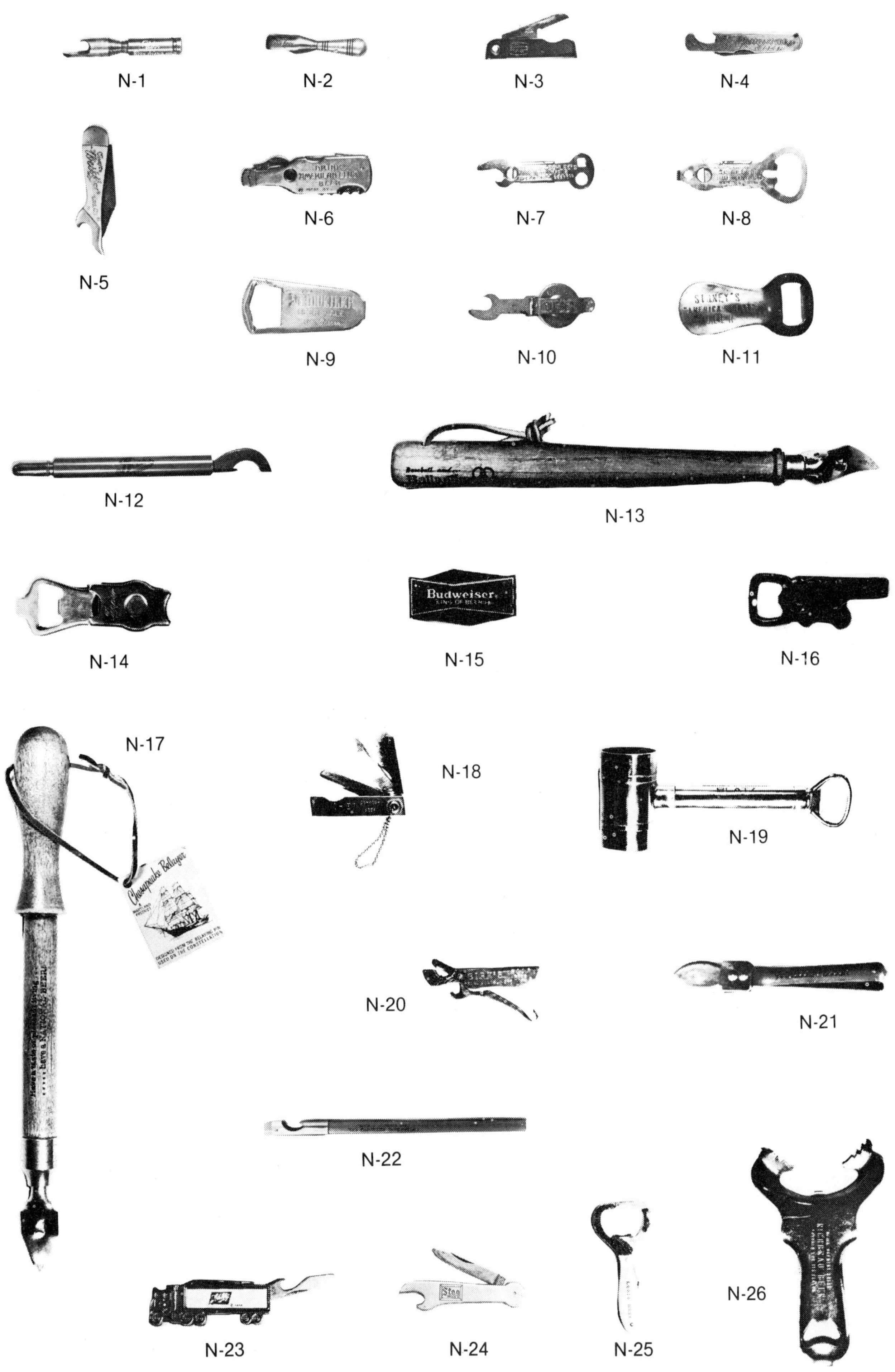

N-1
N-2
N-3
N-4
N-5
N-6
N-7
N-8
N-9
N-10
N-11
N-12
N-13
N-14
N-15
N-16
N-17
N-18
N-19
N-20
N-21
N-22
N-23
N-24
N-25
N-26

TYPE N NOVELTY OPENERS (cont.)

N-27 10″   Combination cap lifter and floating fish knife. Marked "Warco, Stainless Steel, Japan." Reported only with advertising for Ballantine Beer.   15

N-28 3″   Same as N-20 except does not have button hook.   25

N-29 4 5/8″   Combination cap lifter and pencil (bullet end pulls out for pencil). Made by G. Felsenthal & Sons, Chicago.   15

N-30 2 3/4″   Cap lifter and bottle sealer. 2 5/8″ cap lifter slides into plastic sleeve.   8

N-31 2 3/8″   Cap lifter and bottle sealer. This was the only type opener produced by Teraco, Inc. of Midland, Texas. It was sold exclusively with advertising imprinted from 1968 to 1974. More than half a million of them were produced and marketed under the name "Snap A Cap."   12

N-32 3 3/4″   Fishing lure made by Heddon Co. Has both cap lifter and can piercer. Patent No. 2,986,812 was granted on June 6, 1961 for this fishing lure and can opener. The inventors were William Arter Jr. of Shrewsbury, Mass. and Robert G. Clothier of Holden, Mass. Both were employed by Northeast Engineering, Inc. of Worcester, Mass.   7

N-33 3″   Double blade knife/cap lifter made by Empire, Winsted, Conn.   20

N-34 2 5/8″   Cap lifter with single knife blade marked "Latama, Italy."   20

N-35 3″   Cap lifter with single knife blade.   16

N-36 5″   Fish knife with opener on scaler blade. Knife blade marked "Colonial, Pat. No. 2,310,641, U.S.A."   30

N-37 2 1/2″   Key ring knife. 3 blades - opener/screwdriver, knife, and file. Shown in 1980 Stroh's (Detroit) gift catalog for $2.00.

N-38 3 1/8″   Combination cap lifter, screwdriver, nail clipper, and file. Marked Master GSI (in circle) Clipper, U.S. Pat. Pend.   15

N-39 7 1/2″   Stainless knife and fork with opener slide together in plastic handles for storage.   15

TYPE O WALL MOUNT STATIONARY OPENERS

O-1 2 7/8″   wide. Opener mounts with 2 screws.   15

O-2 2 1/8″   wide. Enamelled opener mounts with 4 screws. Made by Erickson Co., Des Moines, Iowa.   12

O-3 2 1/8″   wide. Two piece (plastic and metal) mounts to wall with one screw. Marked "Remembrance, B & B, St. Paul, Minn., U.S.A." About 1957.   12

O-4 2 1/2″   wide. Vaughan's "Never Chip" bottle opener mounts with two screws. Appears in Vaughan's 1922 and 1970 catalogs. Packed in individual boxes which state "It's the only *Stationary* Bottle Opener made which will remove "the cap" without chipping the bottle, it's flexible." On June 18, 1912 Patent No. 1,029,645 was issued to Henry Lockwood Vaughan for this opener.   8

O-5 2 3/4″   wide. The most commonly seen advertising wall mount opener mounts with 2 screws. Made by Brown Manufacturing Co., Inc., of Newport News, Virginia under the registered trademark "Starr." A 1946 advertisement proclaims "The World's Best Opener, Eliminate loss of bottles and contents. Prevent danger to the public. Have long life." Patent No. 2,033,088 was granted to Raymond M. Brown of Newport News and assigned to Brown Mfg. on Nov. 2, 1943. Brown was claiming improvements on Patent No. 1,534,211 issued to Thomas C. Hamilton of Boston, Mass. on Apr. 21, 1925.   6

O-6 2 5/8″   wide. Enamelled opener mounts with 3 screws. Not marked with manufacturer but probably another product of Erickson, Des Moines.   12

O-7 3 3/4″   wide. Metal and plastic opener with bin to catch caps. Made by B & B, St. Paul, Minn.   15

O-8 2″   wide. Opener mounts with 4 screws. On May 7, 1929 Thomas Harding of Newark, New Jersey was granted Patent No. 1,711,678 for this invention. It was assigned to the J.L. Sommer Manufacturing Co. of New Jersey. It was also covered by Canadian Patent No. 289,495.   22

O-9 1 1/4″   wide. Opener mounts with two screws. Opener shown is marked "Walden, Cambridge 28, Mass." and advertising is for Stegmaier Gold Medal Beer, Wilkes-Barre, Pa. The opener is depicted in a 1961 Handy-Walden, Inc. (New York) catalog and is called "Wal-Ope."   18

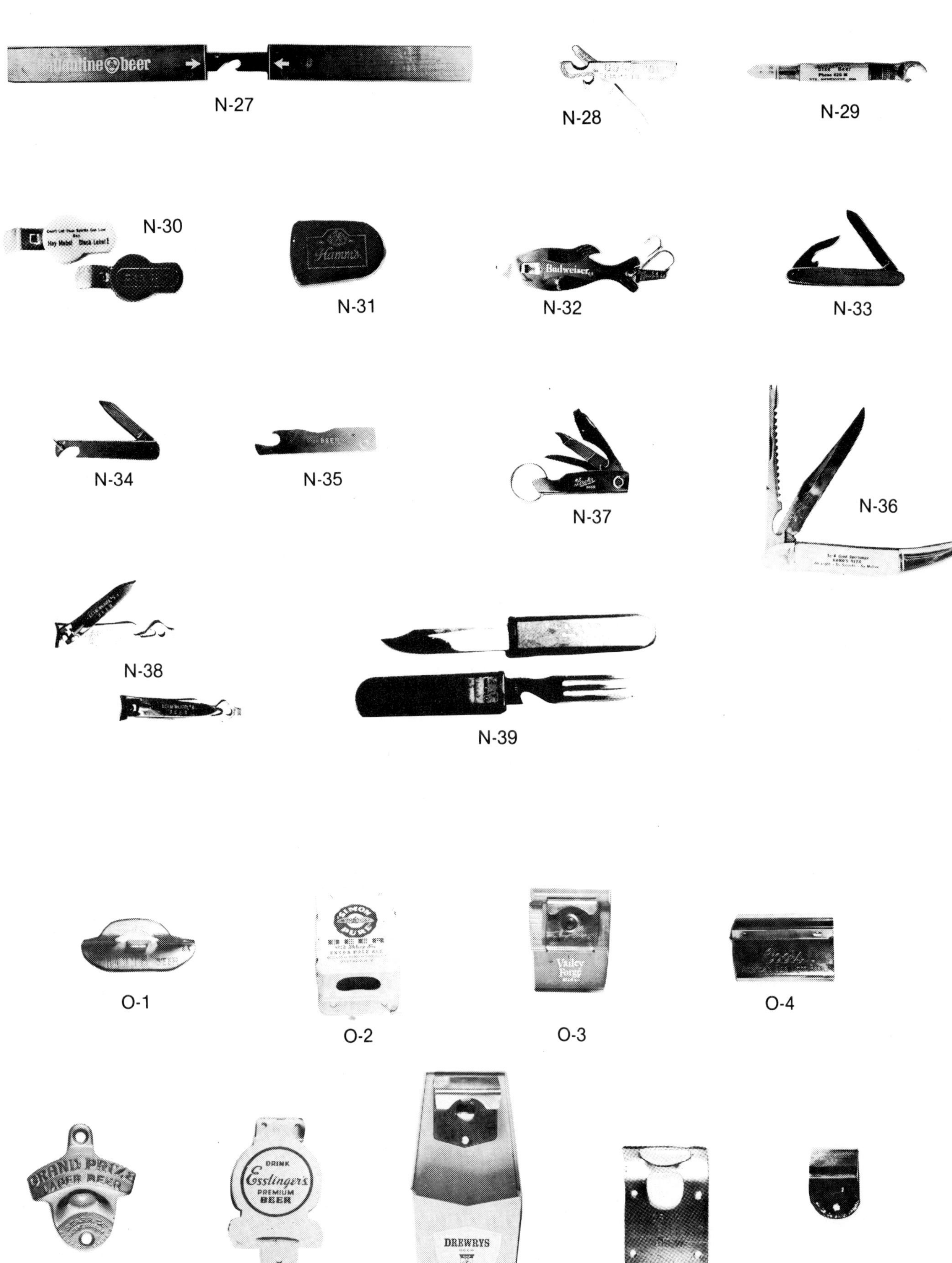

N-27

N-28

N-29

N-30

N-31

N-32

N-33

N-34

N-35

N-37

N-36

N-38

N-39

O-1

O-2

O-3

O-4

O-5

O-6

O-7

O-8

O-9

TYPE P CORKSCREWS

Corkscrews played an important role in beer advertising and as a necessary tool in the 1800's and into the 1900's. Some corkscrews are shown under types listed earlier. An additional 34 are shown on the following two photo pages. They are grouped by similarities and will be discussed in order of appearance on the pages. There are a number of variations on some of these types and only the easily distinguishable variations are shown.

P-1   Patented by W.R. Clough Feb. 1, 1876 (#172,868). This corkscrew has been reported in 3″ and 4″ lengths and 2 7/8″ and 3 1/8″ handle widths. It appears in an 1887 C.T. Williamson Co. (New Jersey) catalog as a "Duplex Power Cork Screw" steel wire, double and twisted shank with wire handle. The second or short screw upon entering the cork put great pressure on the cork causing it to turn in the bottle. Continuing to turn it and slightly pulling it would result in easy extraction. Shown in an advertisement for Anheuser-Busch Brewing Association at $24.00 per gross (144).   30

P-8   Wood handle corkscrew. Edwin Walker patent No. 501,975 of July 25, 1893.   15-25

P-9   Same as above with cast iron crown cap lifter in handle.   20-25

P-10   Wood handle corkscrew. Edwin Walker patent No. 647,775 of April 17, 1900. Walker had incorporated the wire breaker and cap lifter into the cast "bell" (piece on the shank).   14-20

P-12   Wood handle corkscrew with "Decapitator" and wood protective sleeve for the screw. The "Decapitator" was covered by patent No. 950,509 of March 1, 1910, issued to William R. Clough.   15-20

P-13   Wood handle corkscrew. Made by Erie Specialty Manufacturing Co. (1888-1891) for Schlitz Brewing Co. The handle and the bell both depict the Schlitz globe symbol.   20

P-17   Wood handle corkscrew with wire breaker. The small washer and cotter pin retainer above the bell was a W.A. Williamson patent of Aug. 10, 1897 (No. 579,200)   20-25

P-22   Wood handle corkscrew without bell, manufactured by Williamson.   15-20

P-24   Wood handle corkscrew by Williamson. Handle is flat both sides.   18-22

P-32   Wood handle corkscrew.   25

P-2   The "Davis" corkscrew. Patented by D.W. Davis, July 14, 1891, No. 455,826.   25

P-20   Corkscrew with cap lifter marked "Bottle-Boy." Made in U.S.A. by A & J.   12

P-21   Corkscrew with cap lifter and wire cutter blade. Made by Universal Cutlery Co., Switzerland.   15

P-23   Combination cap lifter, can opener, and corkscrew. Patented by C.G. Taylor Dec. 25, 1906. Unusual to see a beer advertisement on this type - The Gutsch Brewing Co.   25

One of the most significant factors in the development of the corkscrew was Edwin Walker of Erie, Pa. who appropriately dubbed his wood handled invention the "Self-Puller." The key was the method of retaining the bell on the shank and the subsequent features Walker incorporated into the bell. In 1896 he added the wire cutter blade to the bell frame, and in 1900 he added the cap lifter in the bell by removing a portion of the frame. He had designed the self-pulling, wire-breaking, and cap lifting features into a single unit. As a result, production costs were cut and the Walker Bell was a useful and very saleable product at an affordable price for many a beer advertiser.

Types P-20, P-21, P-27, and P-28 are often referred to as "Waiters' Tools."

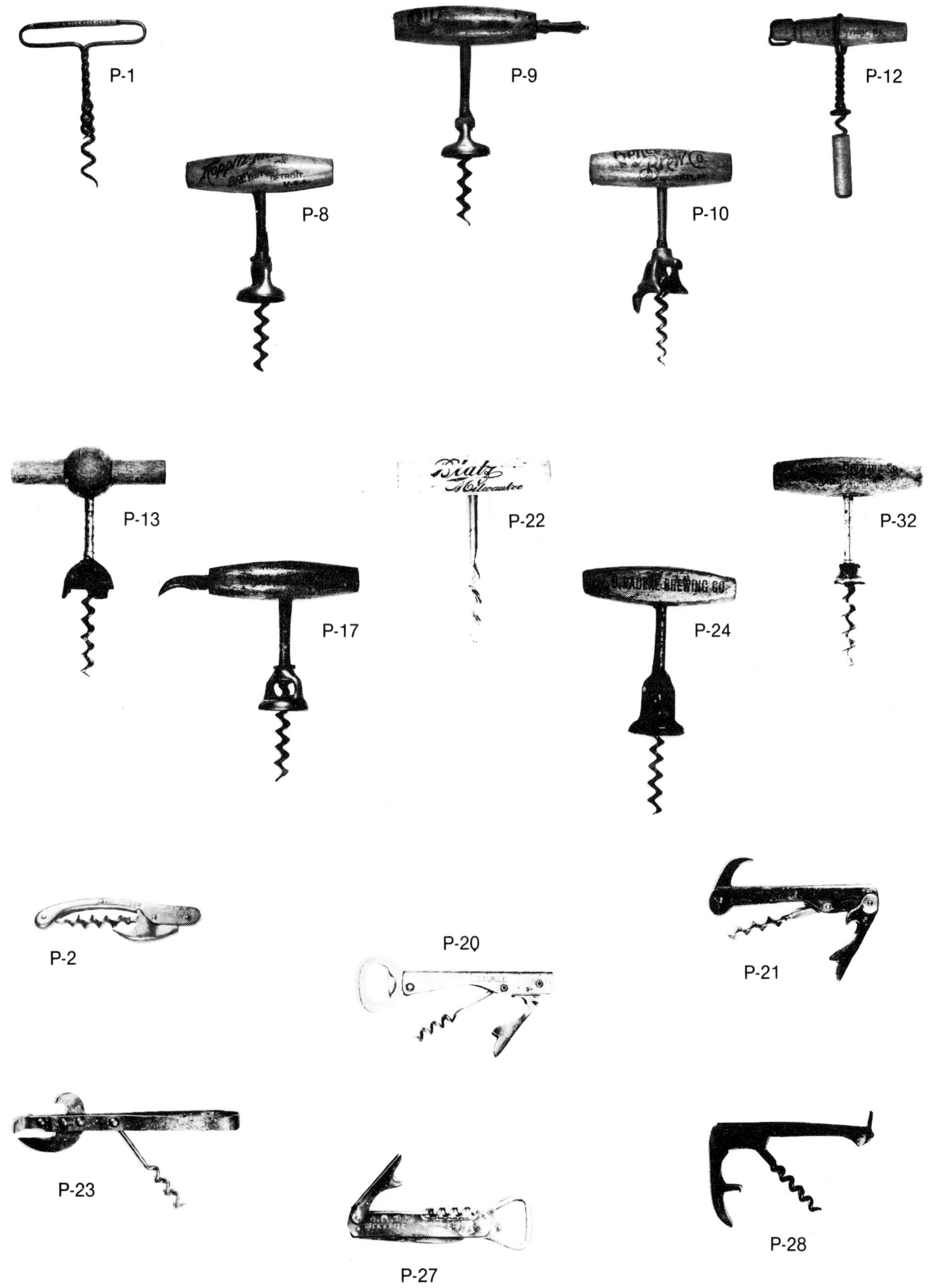

P-1
P-8
P-9
P-10
P-12
P-13
P-17
P-22
P-24
P-32
P-2
P-20
P-21
P-23
P-27
P-28

TYPE P CORKSCREWS (cont.)

Listed in order by appearance on the photo page. See introduction to Type P Corkscrews on page 34.

P-3   Folding corkscrew patented by Carl Hollweg of Barmen, Germany, Feb. 24, 1891, Patent No. 447,185.   40

P-4   Very unusal combination of cap lifter with bell and corkscrew in wood sleeve. Marked "Sequoia Beer, Phone 37391."   45

P-11   Clamshell corkscrew manufactured by Williamson Co., Newark, New Jersey under brand name "Tip Top." Only beer advertising noted for this type is "Salinas Brewing Company, Monterey Beer."   40

P-5   Pocket corkscrew in metal sleeve. Double twisted steel wire construction. A later version of Clough's 1876 patent (see type P-1).   30

P-6   Cap lifter and corkscrew in wooden sleeve.   20

P-18   Cap lifter with wire breaker and corkscrew in metal sleeve.   25

P-19   Double ring wire handle corkscrew (Clough patent) in wooden sleeve.   20

P-31   Like P-18 except has wooden sleeve.   20

P-7   Double ring wire handle corkscrew in wooden sleeve with cap lifter. Several different markings appear on the sleeve of this corkscrew. Those noted from Berghoff, Burkhardt, and Birkenhauer Brewing Companies are marked "A.W. Stephens Mfg. Co., Waltham, Mass., Pat. *Apr. 30, 1901.*" Another from Robert Smith Ale Brewing Co. is marked "A.W. Stephens Mfg. Co., Pat. *Mar. 30, 1901.*" And finally one from the Atz Brewery, Egg Harbor City, New Jersey is marked "N. Simmons, New York City, Pat. *Apr. 30, 1910.*" The Smith Ale Brewing Co. is dated at 1916 by the fact that it states "Famous for 142 Years" and "Established 1774."   20-25

P-33   Cap lifter with wire breaker and corkscrew like P-18. In wooden sleeve with ice pick.   25

P-14   Corkscrew, knife, cap lifter combination. Mother of pearl handles. Some marks noted: "Camco, U.S.A." "Kent, N.Y.C." "Colonial, Prov., R.I."   16-20

P-15   Corkscrew, cap lifter, single knife blade combination.   16-20

P-16   Corkscrew, cap lifter, double knife blades combination. Made by Imperial Knife Company, Providence, R.I.   25-30

P-25   Combination corkscrew, double blade knife, cap lifter, and wire breaker. Has a small hole with magnifier which serves to view a photo when held up to the light. The example shown here is from Bergner & Engel Brew. Co. and a trademark of the company can be seen when looking through the peephole. Complete with photo these openers are rare. There are reportedly 48 variations (in color, design, etc.) of this type for Anheuser-Busch. Values vary widely depending on condition.   60-300

P-26   Corkscrew with two knife blades and wire breaker. The example shown has very ornate handles including a scene of the American Brewing Co. factory in Philadelphia. Beautiful and ornate pieces exist in all types of handles - silver, pearl, ivory, etc.   60-300

P-29   Corkscrew, knife blade, file blade, wire cutter blade, and cigar cutter.   75-120

P-34   Corkscrew, 2 knife blades, and wire cutter. Mother of pearl handles.   60-90

P-30   This corkscrew mounts on the edge of a bar with three screws. The bottle is held under the overhang and the screw is turned into the cork by rotating the top handle. The lever is then raised and the cork is extracted. It was invented by Edwin Walker of Erie, Pa. and Patent No. 452,625 was issued May 19, 1891.   80-150

For additional corkscrews see the following types: A-36, B-13, B-35, B-36, B-38, C-26, F-21, G-3, G-10, H-4, H-10, L-2, L-6, M-23, M-25, M-26, M-39, M-53, N-6, and N-19.

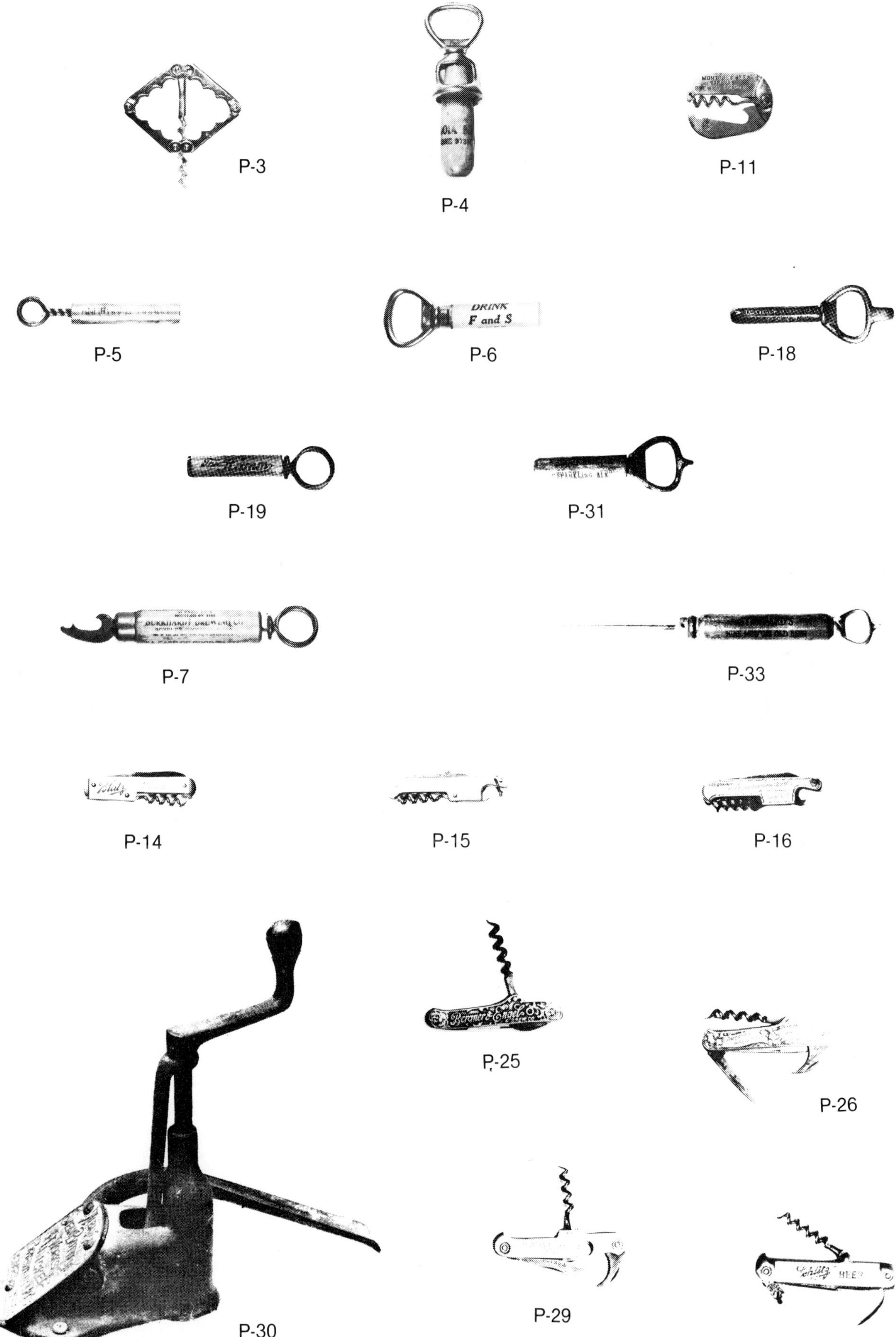

P-3
P-4
P-11
P-5
P-6
P-18
P-19
P-31
P-7
P-33
P-14
P-15
P-16
P-30
P-25
P-26
P-29
P-34

TYPE Q ROUND PLASTIC OPENERS

Q-1   3 3/4″ diameter. Opener for push tab cans. Place on top of can, press down, and tabs are depressed.   2
Q-2   2 1/4″ diameter. Opener for twist off bottle caps. Serrated edges aid hand grip.   2
Q-3   2 1/2″ diameter. Metal piece with opener attached to underside of plastic shell with screws.   3

TYPE R FIGURALS

Types R-1 through R-4 are from the period 1954-1955 and are marked either Iroquois Beverage Corp. or International Breweries, Inc. - this was the period in which the name change was taking place. Reportedly there were ten different little Indians made . . . an eleventh was reported in Jan. 1981. They are as follows:

R-1   4 1/2″   Red plastic with metal cap lifter. Two varieties - one for each name Iroquois and International.   8
R-2   3 3/8″   Tin and steel - flat on back. Two varieties for Iroquois Beverage Corp. - Bronze tone and chocolate color.   10
R-3   4 3/4″   Free standing three dimensional figure. 6 varieties: Two different metals - Magnesium and Aluminum each with two imprint variations - ''Iroquois Bev. Corp. Buffalo, N.Y.'' on three lines and ''Iroquois Beverage Corp., Buffalo, N.Y.'' of five lines. Imprint on the back. Fifth variety is painted brown, black, red, and yellow and have five line imprint. The sixth variety (and the eleventh Indian reported) is cast in brass.   20-40
R-4   5″   The rarest of the Indians. Opener top is hinged for storage of matches inside. There is no advertising imprint.   60
R-5   7″   Figural shark cast in aluminum - mouth is opener. Frequently seen with no advertising. Example has Schlitz logo.   20
R-6   6 1/4″   Wall mounted opener from Sprenger Brewing Co., Lancaster, Pa. depicts brewmaster with mug of beer. Made in brass (90-120) and painted cast iron (100-150)
R-7   2 7/8″   Cast iron pretzel. Open is in top ring.   20-25
R-8   6 3/4″   Wall mounted painted cast iron opener from Kaier Brewing Co., Mahanoy City, Pa. depicts coal miner with pick and mug of beer. Rare.   180-250

TYPE S BOTTLE BOTTLE OPENERS

S-1   5 3/4″ high bottle with opener formed in glass in the bottom (one would need two bottles to open one). These were produced by the Fair Mount Glass Co. of Indianapolis, Indiana in 1958, Patent #2,992,574 was later granted to Werner Martinmass of Wayzata, Minnesota on March 18, 1959. The patent is fairly interesting and amusing to read (not dry and boring like so many such documents). Here is an excerpt from the patent: ''Containers such as bottles and cans which are provided with a crown cap are a great source of annoyance on accounts of the frequency with which a person finds himself in possession of several containers of a beverage, but no opener for removing their crown caps. A person is particularly likely to find himself in this predicament while fishing, hunting or picnicking. The resulting efforts to remove the crown caps from the containers are likely to cause damage to other articles with which removal of the caps is attempted, or serious injury to the mouth or teeth if one is foolish enough to attempt to remove the caps in that manner.'' The idea of using one container to open another was not new. On June 29, 1943 Gerard Deane of New York was granted patent No. 2,322,843 in which he describes a cone top can with a built-in opener for opening another cone top can.   10-14

TYPE T TAP KNOB OPENERS

T-1 to T-4 The four openers with tap knobs shown here vary in height from 6 3/4″ to 8 1/4″. They are presently being marketed by Anheuser-Busch as part of their ''Clydesdale Collection'' for $14.95 each.

TYPE Z — In a class by itself!

Z - 1 While removing the cap the handle is squeezed and the cap is held in the jaws. Reported only with advertising for Cremo Beer and Ale (New Britian, Conn.) - white lettering on red enamel. The box the opener is packaged in is marked Talbot Products, Inc., New Britain, Conn. The box also bears the Patent No. 780,149 which is the patent number for a Bob Sled Runner issued in 1905. It is called the ''Miracle Opener.''   15

Q-1

Q-2

Q-3

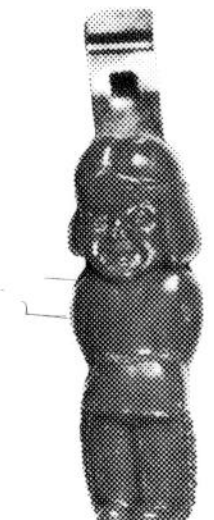

R-1   R-2   R-3   R-4

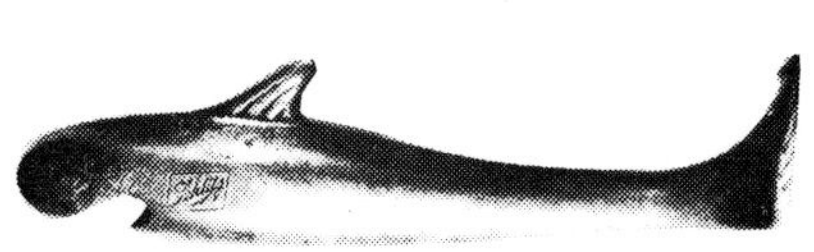

R-5

R-7

R-6

R-8

S-1

T-1   T-2   T-3   T-4

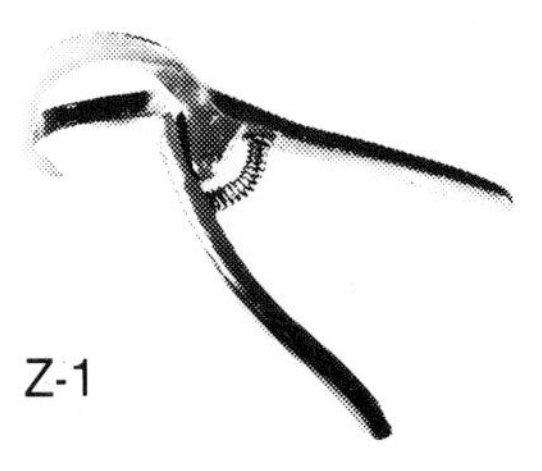

Z-1

Reproduction of 1922 Vaughan Novelty Mfg. Co. Catalog. Although this catalog was issued during prohibition, it is interesting to note the reproduction of beer advertising openers — Schlitz, Schoenhofen, etc. Obviously, these were made prior to the Jan., 1920 effective date of the 18th amendment.

CATALOG and PRICE LIST
No. 25
1922

Vaughan Novelty Mfg. Co.
Incorporated

MANUFACTURERS
—OF—
ADVERTISING NOVELTIES
—AND—
PREMIUMS IN METALS

3211-25 Carroll Avenue
Chicago, Ill., U. S. A.

Vaughan Novelty Mfg. Co.

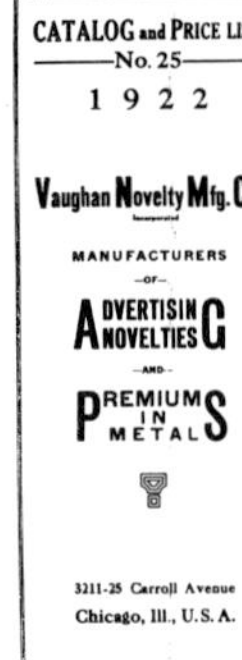

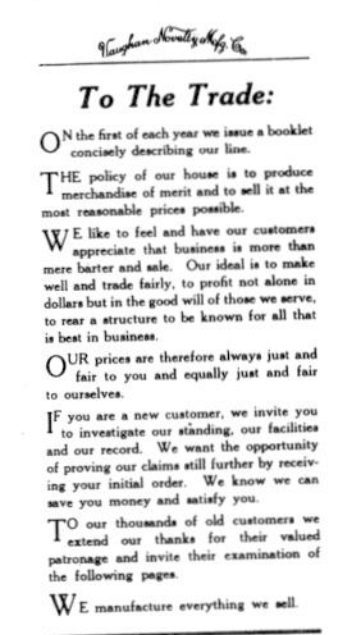

To The Trade:

ON the first of each year we issue a booklet concisely describing our line.

THE policy of our house is to produce merchandise of merit and to sell it at the most reasonable prices possible.

WE like to feel and have our customers appreciate that business is more than mere barter and sale. Our ideal is to make well and trade fairly, to profit not alone in dollars but in the good will of those we serve, to rear a structure to be known for all that is best in business.

OUR prices are therefore always just and fair to you and equally just and fair to ourselves.

IF you are a new customer, we invite you to investigate our standing, our facilities and our record. We want the opportunity of proving our claims still further by receiving your initial order. We know we can save you money and satisfy you.

TO our thousands of old customers we extend our thanks for their valued patronage and invite their examination of the following pages.

WE manufacture everything we sell.

Vaughan Novelty Mfg. Co.
Chicago, U. S. A.

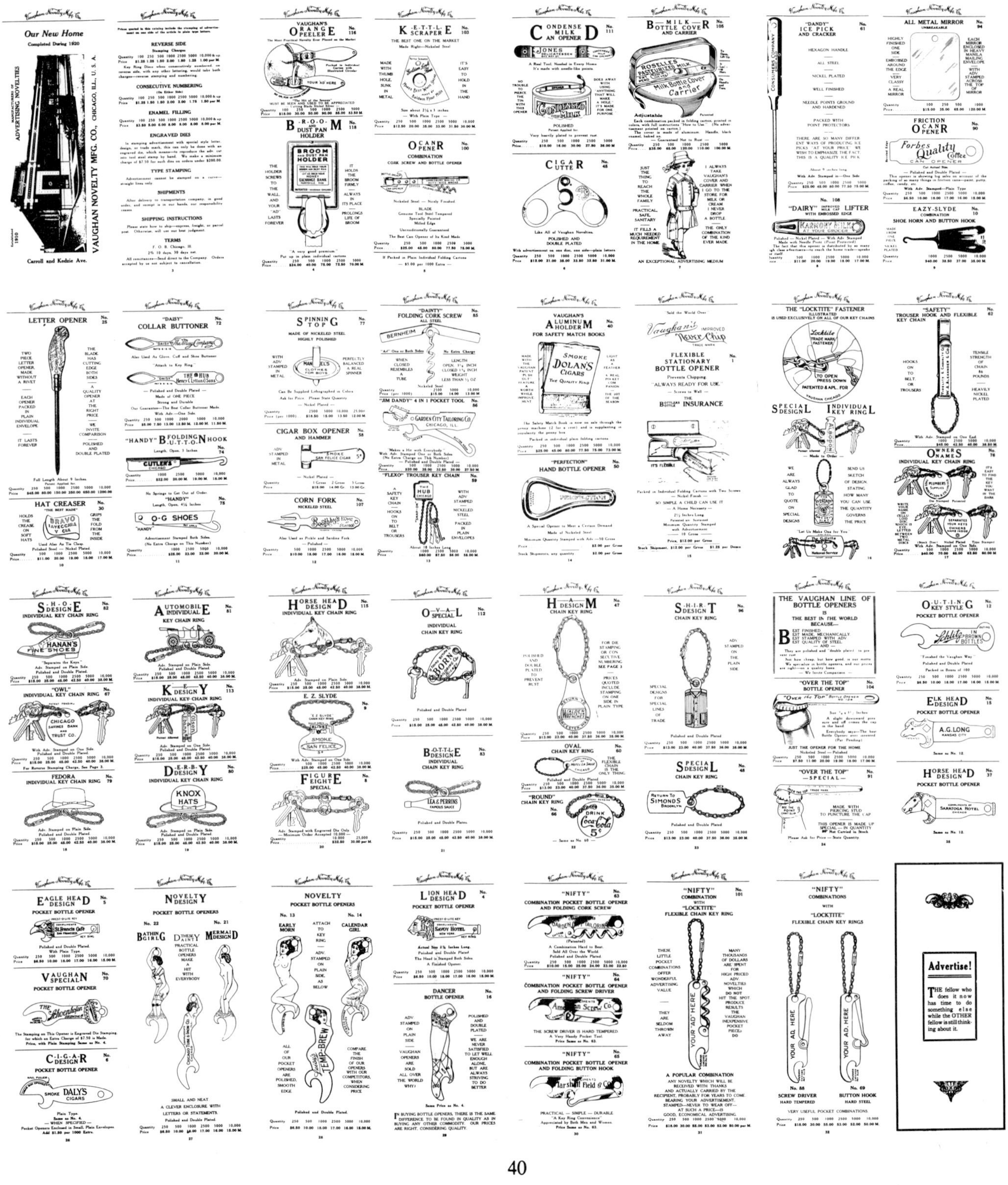